the
thinking
heart

the thinking heart

The Literary Archive of Wilfred Watson

Paul Hjartarson and Shirley Neuman

Bruce Peel Special Collections Library / October 16, 2014 to January 30, 2015

Bruce Peel Special Collections Library
B7 Rutherford South
Edmonton, Alberta, Canada
T6G 2J4

Library and Archives Canada Cataloguing in Publication

Hjartarson, Paul Ivar, author
The thinking heart : the literary archive of Wilfred Watson / Paul Hjartarson and Shirley Neuman.

Includes bibliographical references.
ISBN 978-1-55195-339-7 (PBK.)

1. Watson, Wilfred, 1911–1998. 2. Watson, Wilfred, 1911–1998—Archives. 3. Watson, Wilfred, 1911–1998—Criticism and interpretation. 4. Poets, Canadian (English)—20th century—Biography. 5. Dramatists, Canadian (English)—20th century—Biography. 6. University of Alberta—Faculty—Biography. 7. University of Alberta. Archives. I. Neuman, Shirley, 1946–, author II. University of Alberta. Archives III. University of Alberta. Library, issuing body IV. Title.

PS8545.A885Z85 2014 C811'.54 C2014-905850-0

Design and layout: Lara Minja, Lime Design Inc.
Editorial: Leslie Vermeer
Digital reproduction: Nicholas van Orden
Exhibition installation: Carol Irwin

First edition, first printing, 2014
Printed in Canada by McCallum Printing Group Inc.

contents

The making of a will has been on my mind. . . .

I'd like to leave my papers to some person or some institution . . . as throwing light on the probing eclecticism of my mind and art. It is said that Leonardo da Vinci introduced a new probing-kind of drawing, in which the artist's pencil traces the path of his perception over and over again, probing that perception. When I started to draw as a hobby, I wd. keep at a sketch until I'd destroyed it. There is an emblematic fact here, about my writing in general. The Jews loved god so much, that when he appeared amongst them, they crucified him, not thinking that he was god, but in their love of him thinking he was an imposter. In this sense, I have crucified my talent, not because I distrusted it, but to prove it. I think there is an analogy here for knowledge. To know is to eclectisize and to challenge, even to destruction, what is gathered from all kinds of sources. I expect my papers to show this process developing. (91-238 May 19 1979)[1]

Early Life

In January 1955 T.S. Eliot accepted Wilfred Watson's first book of poetry, *Friday's Child*, for publication at Faber and Faber (SW-570).[2] Sheila Watson had submitted the manuscript on her husband's behalf in what appears to have been a bold response to the rejection of poems Watson himself had offered to a number of literary magazines in the fall of 1953 and, possibly, to McClelland and Stewart.[3] *Friday's Child* would earn Watson the 1955 Governor General's Literary Award for Poetry and the British Arts Council Poetry Prize.

This coup surely came as a surprise to Canadian writers and readers for Watson, now forty-four, had previously published little: three poems in *The Canadian Forum* written in the context of war and published between November 1939 and June 1940,[4] then nothing until summer 1951 when Alan Crawley published in *Contemporary Verse* seven poems that Watson would include in *Friday's Child* and the uncollected "Litter." When he submitted more poems to *Contemporary Verse* in early 1952,[5] Crawley accepted only "Queen of Tarts," rejecting the rest as "heavy handed, lacking in vitality, giving a feeling of striving by the writer and slightly unimportant just at this time" (95-309 Crawley to WW Mar 28 1952). After that, *Fiddlehead* took "An Admiration for Dylan Thomas."[6] These were the poems by which his Canadian audience knew him, when T.S. Eliot, attempting to raise interest in the forthcoming collection, facilitated the

Wilfred Watson, aged about fifteen; unidentified photographer (95-24-16)

appearance of "Graveyard on a Cliff of White Sand" in *The London Magazine* and of "A Contempt for Dylan Thomas" and "The Ballad of Mother and Son" in *The Paris Review*.[7]

The *Canadian Forum* poems betray the influence of T.S. Eliot's Modernism, which Watson knew through anthologies (91-252 Feb 19 1981)[8] and which he understood through the eyes and ears of a Canadian West Coast writer. "Lines for the Twenty-fifth Anniversary of the Declaration of War, August 4, 1914" raises the ghost of Prufrock: the evening silence "disdains" even the "swish of the / returning cars" and becomes "an obdurate sullen thing" with "a fascination / like a cloud of chlorine gas." The typists of "Compartments" also belong to the world of Prufrock,

> . . . chatting of dates and marriages,
>
> Of the latest shades of stockings cobweb-sheer,
> Of the boss's incompetency and aversions,
> Of Hedy Lamarr's precision of gender,
> Of what the Germans did and what the Russians. . . .

Lieutenant Frederick Walter
Watson, RCN
retired 3 Oct. 1944

29 May 1925 permission
given to proceed to
Vancouver, B.C.
addressed to
Mr. F.W. Watson Gunner (T)
RN.
Burgfield
Cold Norton
Latchingdon
Chelmsford.

Retired 24 June 1920

Record of Frederick Watson's retirement from the British Royal Navy in 1920, and of "permission" to emigrate, 1925; notes in Sheila Watson's hand (95-16)

Facing page: A memory of England from a draft of an unpublished introduction to *Plays at the Iron Bridge* (91-450)

A repeated refrain describes the "Armed Merchantman" as an "old cow of a ship" filled with "faces white as uncooked pastry," each looking homeward, each exhibiting a thoroughly Modernist alienation.

That Wilfred Watson should in his late twenties have been publishing Modernist poetry in *The Canadian Forum* was anything but a foregone conclusion. Born in Rochester, England, on May 1, 1911, he was one of three children of Louisa Claydon and Frederick Walter Watson, a "leading seaman" who during World War I "had joined the crew of the H.M.S. Valiant," then returned, without conspicuous success, to civilian life, settling in Cold Norton. Watson attended nearby Maldon Grammar School as a scholarship boy; there he began the reading of Shakespeare that he continued for the rest of his life.[9] When he was fourteen,[10] the family emigrated, settling in Duncan on Vancouver Island. Watson attended school for one year then, for lack of a local high school, took a job at the Chemainus sawmill. In a late poem, "portrait of myself as a

The auto-biography of Tom Horror/ the birth of W.W.

WILFRED Watson was born in Rochester, Kent, England at 14 Horseby Road, according to his birth certificate which he had copied in 1978: May 1st, 1911. His father is said to be "Frederick Walter Watson" , his mother, Louisa, both of whom were the thirteenth children of their respective families. He was the first-born to both of them -- there is a small irony in this fact. His father is said to be a 'leading seaman' -- another small irony. But the approaching holocaust of the first world war no doubt welcomed those who as Frederick Walter Watson showed marked promise of success in gunnery, torpedoes, mines, diving, electrical ciruitry, and a renewed technology . By the time this smart 'leading seaman' had joined the crew of H.M.S. Valiant as its book-keeping officer in charge of its electrical circuits and its torpedoes he had also found time to beget a second child, a daughter, who was named Joan. He had spent two years on a destroyer , which had taken him around the world, and been rewarded for his services with an office and aplace in the warrant officer's mess. This seemed palatial to young Wilfred when he was taken aboard, though he was more interested in the long climb down the tube to see the ship's torpedoes. The latter

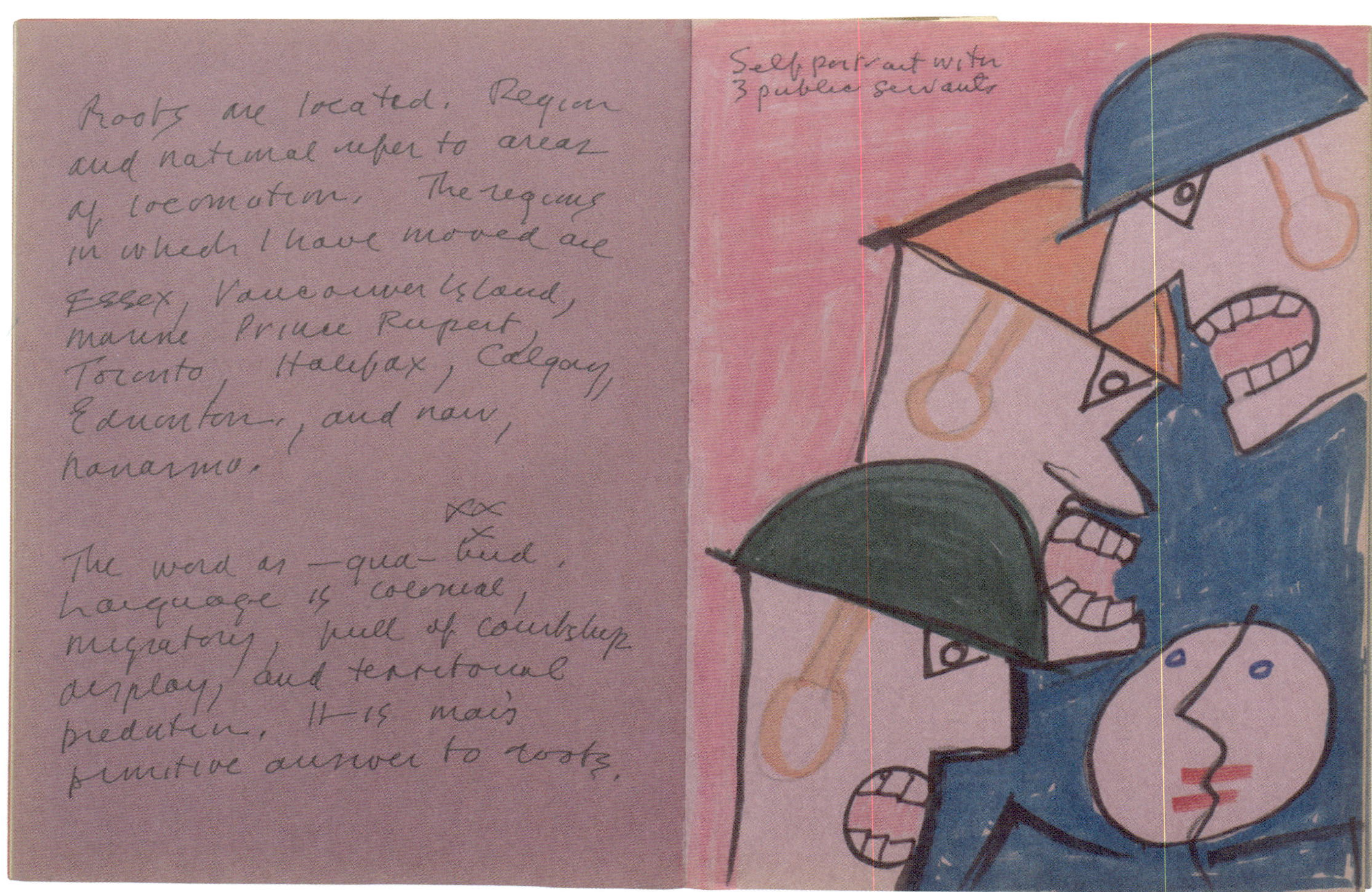
Roots are located. Region and national refer to areas of locomotion. The regions in which I have moved are Essex, Vancouver Island, Prince Rupert, Toronto, Halifax, Calgary, Edmonton, and now, Nanaimo.
The word as — qua — bird. Language is colonial, migratory, full of courtship display, and territorial predation. It is man's primitive answer to roots.
Self portrait with 3 public servants

On moving back to the West Coast in 1980, Watson drew many "portraits" with "chain saw" teeth. They represented those who destroyed the environment, but also those who made life miserable — public servants enforcing regulations, Job's cruel comforters, among others (91-266).

freshman" on the Chemainus "campus," he would enumerate his "courses" in the head saw, the circular saw, the trim saw, repeated for fourteen years until "my mind 8 began to / 9 crack" (91-259 Mar 30 1981).

We have scant documentation of this period of his life. What we do know suggests that, despite the grind of the sawmill, he led a rich intellectual and creative life. In "portrait of myself as a freshman," he recalls beginning to read Spinoza, "Mill on Liberty," Havelock Ellis, Malinowski on "the north Melanesian savages," T.S. Eliot, and William Empson. A photograph, either lost or displaced in the archive, and an early poem, "For R.H. Halhed and E. Hart" (91-389), attest to a group of friends with whom he hiked and picnicked at Mount Arrowsmith outside Port Alberni.[11] He became friends with Dorothy Bazett, a Duncan schoolteacher with lively literary and musical interests, and with Jeannette Cann, who taught English and philosophy at Victoria College until 1938, corresponding with both until their deaths. He and the West Coast

Watson drew this figure many times during the 1980s, often as a portrait of the "victim" of the men with chain saw teeth (95-OS1-479).

"Witch on Cow Back," a theme in Watson's drawings of the early 1980s (95-OS2-182)

For R.H. Halhed and E. Hart

The sun unrisen; we left Cameron Lake and at a pace
Not fast, not slow, up through the dark cool woods
Through shadow and silence, in our bloods'
Silence, we moved up to the mountain face:
In an hour we entered a green paradise
Where like archangels of wood, a wood crowds
Down to a creek; we drink where July floods
Dwindle in August stones; now the sun's rays
Kindle our noon high path; we are bit by flies
From warm and damp flying free; our lungs
Grow taut; our limbs begin to weigh; now rise
Before us stinging cliffs of brush, where rungs
Of root lift up our bodies through a drag of boughs;
Further; and then a place of flowering, where
The rock's naked face and snowy brow show bare.

"For R.H. Halhed and E. Hart" (91-389), probably written prior to summer 1940

Watson and Jack Shadbolt, Vancouver, late August 1956; unidentified photographer (95-24-16)

painter Jack Shadbolt became lifelong friends and correspondents, from perhaps as early as September 1928 when Shadbolt began a two-year appointment teaching art in the Duncan school (Scott Watson, 5). It may have been through either Shadbolt or Helen Ruth Humphrey that he saw his first Modernist art, "two or three" paintings by Emily Carr; both knew the painter. Humphrey, then Head of English at Victoria College and another dear friend, edited Carr's letters, and, Watson claimed, "helped" her "transform only partially shaped art sketches into the short stories later published as Klee Wyck, The Book of Small, etc." For Watson, Carr's paintings were an epiphany. "At the same time as I was respondg powerfully to the Vanc. Is. environment, I came by the greatest good fortune across these paintings which 'said' what I had neither words nor technique to say," he would recollect (91-217 Sept 22 1975). This moment, which he recalled as having "preceded my discovery of the Waste Land by several years," was the moment he "first became a modernist" (91-298 draft letter to Shirley Neuman Mar 6 1983).

Watson remembers himself, aged twenty-nine ("remembering the nineteen-forties," *I Begin with Counting*)

remembering the nineteen-forties

portrait 1 of
myself 2 aged
twenty-nine 3 with
ten 4 million
deaths 5 screaming
in 6 my
ears 7 an
atheist 8 without
9 any

friends 1 a
slave 2 without
a 3 soul
trying 4 to
find 5 out
why 6 I
was 7 devastated
by 8 the
9 cry

from 1 a
beach-full 2 of
herons 3 and
seagulls 4 concerning
the 5 wet
slap-slap 6 of
the 7 spade
of 8 the
9 grave-digger

sea. 1 Why,
said 2 eternity
screaming 3 at
me 4 out
of 5 an
abandoned 6 cook-house
full 7 of
wasp 8 nests,
9 why

don't 1 you
invent 2 a
new 3 jesus?
and 4 perhaps
I 5 will,
I 6 answered,
and 7 perhaps
I 8 will
9 set

up 1 a
new 2 church
in 3 an
abandoned 4 slaughter-house.
But 5 you
haven't 6 any
writing-skills, 7 you
can't 8 speak,
9 you

can't 1 even
think, 2 said
eternity 3 mocking
me 4 from
the 5 deck
of 6 an
aircraft 7 carrier
launched 8 at
9 false

creek, 1 vancouver,
bc. 2 Portrait
of 3 myself
aged 4 twenty-nine
portrait 5 of
myself 6 aged
twenty-nine 7 going
on 8 thirty,
9 period.

"Metaxu": drawing of charred driftwood, painted by Watson and named after Simone Weil's use of the Greek word for a bridge between earth and heaven to signify transcendence (91-306)

Below:
Driftwood "heads" with the "chain saw" teeth of a developer; unidentified photographer (91-24-59)

Fragmentary scraps in the archive speak to an artistic ambition far outstripping his circumstances. "At that time, in the thirties, I wasn't sure whether I wanted to be a writer or a painter or a composer," Watson remembered (91-217 Sept 22 1975). There is no evidence that he read music or played an instrument although he listened to classical music with intense appreciation and sometimes thought about his work in terms of musical form. All his life he drew and painted with a freedom of expression he perhaps learned from Shadbolt, and, once he moved to Piper's Lagoon, just north of Nanaimo, in 1980, he began to collect pieces of driftwood on the beach and to use acrylic paint to transform them into "heads." He wrote nearly every day.

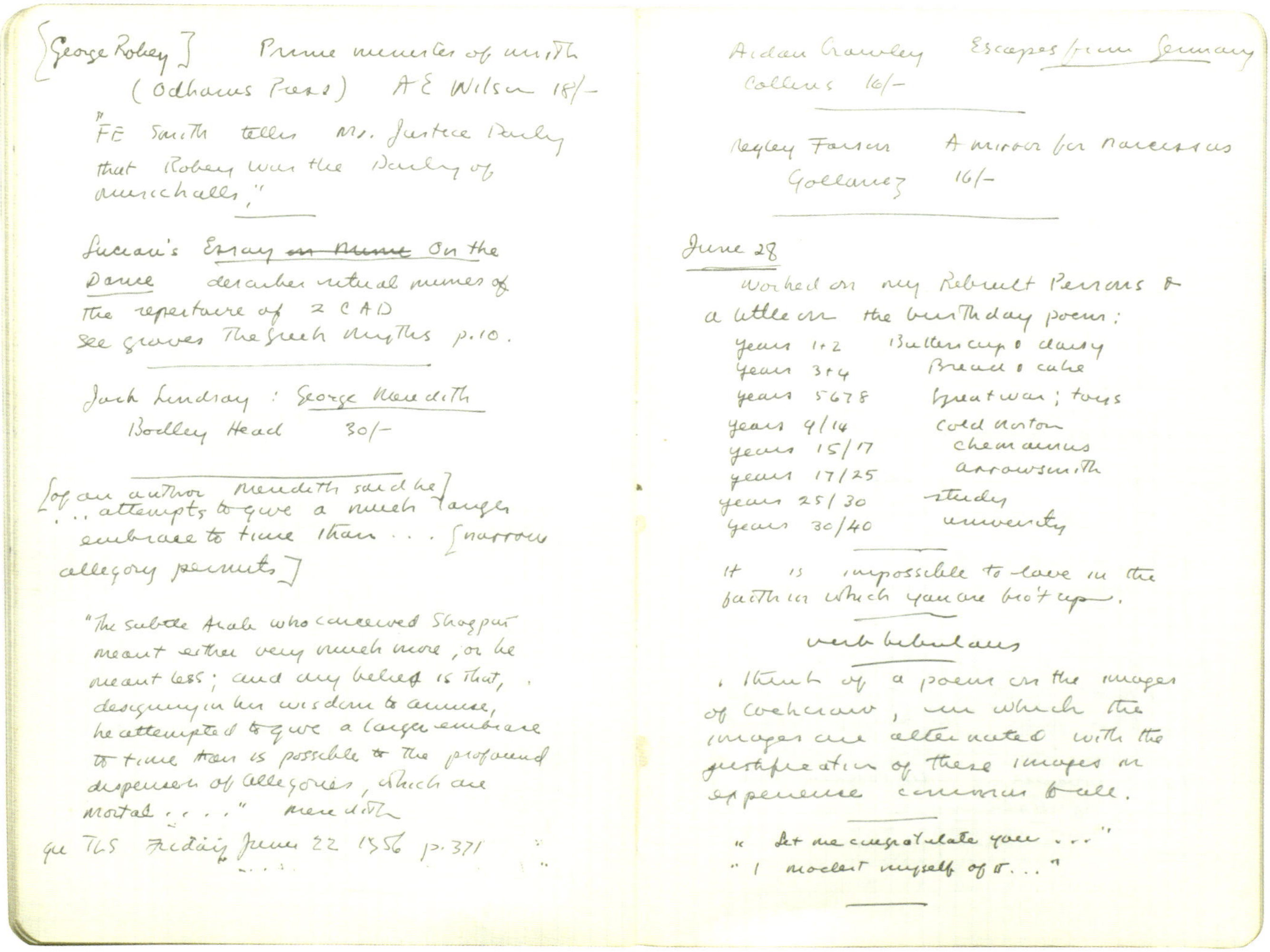

Journal entry outlining "Birthday Poem," 1956 (91-17)

One tantalizing testimony to his early ambition is a chronology he drafted when working on a "birthday poem" (91-17 June 28 1956). There he annotated his fifteenth to seventeenth years, "Chemainus," but his seventeenth through twenty-fifth years, spent working at the sawmill, he named after a mountain, "Arrowsmith." For Watson "mountain" symbolized "artist." When he drafted this chronology he had already been working for several years on a play, "Vision of Entrances," set in a symbolic landscape of the dead, with its mountain of artists, desert of philosophers, swamp of scholars, city of reason, and hill of joy. By age seventeen, Wilfred Watson already thought of himself as an artist.

Autodidact and Undergraduate

His was no mean ambition. In a very rough draft of an unpublished introduction for *Plays at the Iron Bridge*, he recalled: "When I came to Canada . . . I brought with me one ambition, to rewrite Shakespeare's plays, in prose. Much as I admired Shakespeare's poetry, I thought of it as a terrible obstacle to the appreciation of his drama. . . . It was T.S. Eliot who first convinced me I was wrong; that the real problem of drama, as opposed to theatre, was the discovery of an appropriate verse form" (95-120). What he had to guide him was his own truncated education, and his reading and writing of poetry. "His complete and consuming passion is poetry," Sheila Watson wrote in a draft letter to Eliot. "His whole life is turned to it as to the sun" (SW-570).

At age twenty-five, still working, he resumed his education. Between June 1936 and June 1940, he completed his senior matriculation and first-year university courses at Victoria College, then affiliated with the University of British Columbia. In the fall of 1940, Watson moved to Vancouver and enrolled at the University of British Columbia. During that academic year he met Sheila Doherty; they married in December 1941. His work towards his First-Class Honours B.A. in English language and literature, typically for the time, emphasized historical coverage, especially of the earlier periods. He was atypical in his interest in Canadian literature. At a time when Canadian literature was taught as an appendage to American literature courses, he took up the challenge of a prize offered by Dorothy and William Dorbils for the "best essay on a subject on Canadian literature," winning fifty dollars. We do not know his topic.

His third year included a strong focus on Shakespeare. He took two courses with Professor Garnet Sedgwick: the first a "detailed study" of five Shakespeare plays, including *King Lear* and *Hamlet*, with lectures on "Shakespeare's development, his use of sources, and on his relation to the stage and the dramatic practice of his time," the second an honours seminar that focused on "the literature of the 1590s." He also took "Drama to 1642," the "main subject" of which was Elizabethan drama from its "beginnings in the Miracle and Morality" play to its development in Shakespeare's predecessors, its culmination in Shakespeare, and its "decline" in his successors. This intense focus on Renaissance drama, and particularly on Shakespeare, culminated in his bachelor's essay, "Shakespeare's Use of Courtly Love Conventions."[12] The autodidact who had dreamed of rewriting Shakespeare had set out to learn how Shakespeare did it in the first place.

Watson, during his time at UBC; Artona, Vancouver, photographer (95-24-01)

Facing page, top: "What is Shakespeare's dramatic craft?"; journal entry June 28 1960 (91-37)

Facing page, bottom: One of dozens of scenarios derived from Shakespeare to be found in Watson's notebooks (91-269)

Rewriting Shakespeare

Watson would return to Shakespeare throughout his life, much as Shakespeare had turned to earlier sources, rewriting them to speak to his own time. As he was completing the final drafts of his first full-length play, *Cockcrow and the Gulls,* he warned himself:

> It is fatal to accept the crafts of the past as adequate. The first thing a dramatist shd. do is ask what is Shakespeare's dram. craft? But his second quest is, how is that craft inadequate to the present day task. (91-37 June 28 1960)

His notebooks and journals are full of ideas departing from *King Lear, Othello, Anthony and Cleopatra, Hamlet,* and *Measure for Measure.* Those from between 1956 and 1961, for example, include over a dozen scenarios and drafts drawn from Shakespeare. Watson worked extensively on some of these, such as "Karshye, King of All the Russians," based on *King Lear,* which extends over eight notebooks written over more than two years. Twenty years later he was still adapting Shakespeare to his time as in a scenario for a *Hamlet* "deconstruction" with "several ghosts" (91-269 July 6 1981). In *Cockcrow and the Gulls* Higgins is King Lear to Cockcrow's Fool (*Plays*, 30) and is "heaped up full of

problems.

It is fatal to accept the crafts of the past as adequate. The first thing a dramatist shd. do is

ask what is Shakespeare's dram. craft?

But his second quest is, how is that craft inadequate to the present day task. As long as the dramatist feels this craft is adequate, he will not produce great drama. Until he has thoroly investigated it, he will not know whether it is adequate or not.

Now I conceive the problem quite clearly:— it is to show that our world view is inadequate. His world view was totally unlike ours. Yet the formula holds for

tragedy generally. If anything, the formula is more poignant today, because we are the more optimistic. We are more utopian, less optimistic — very pessimistic, in the heroic sense. Thus our tragedy is bound to be non-heroic; utopian rather heroic; domestic rather than political; religious, rather than ethical. For example, *Faustus* is a non-heroic tragedy. It is a utopian tragedy. *A View from the Bridge* fails because it is essentially ethical tragedy. But our optimism doesn't lie in that direction.

Tragedy, as I conceive it, always explores the *hubris* of the age it is written in.

In *mother courage*, the hubris lies with courage. The other

he too is Oedipus.

Monday (06 17 hrs) 6. seven. LXXXI

Deconstructions. A Hamlet in which several ghosts appear with conflicting injunctions to the several persons of the action. — An Oedipus in which Creon, and Tiresias, are guilty of the same crime — innocent crime — as Oedipus.

xx
x

deconstructed 5 by
anouilh 6 blended
by 7 the
intellectual 8 beauty

9 of

her 1 own
mind 2 and
became 3 an 4 Jamesean
Ellen
her 5 tongue
torn 6 out

by 7 the
precision 8 it

9 seeks

x x
x

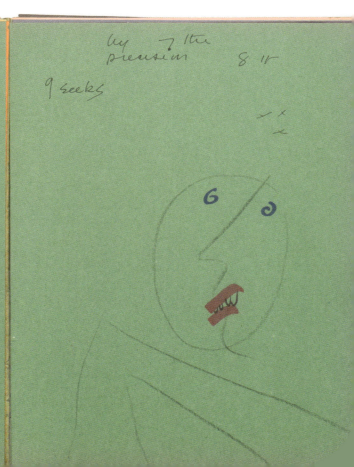

A rough draft explaining the subtitle, "The Autobiography of Tom Horror" (91-117)

readers of Shakespeare
Most ~~people~~ wd
agree that Macbeth's
lines, spoken when he
has just heard of the
death of ~~lady~~ his
wife,

tomorrow and tomorrow and
tomorrow
Creeps on this petty pace
from day to day

are without question ~~the~~ perhaps
supreme utterance. Wilfred
Watson in punning on these
words is renewing them
diacronically from the
cliché they have by their
mastery aged into: If so
by directing his attention
from the Macbeth / the
Macbeth become cliché /
Macbeth become archetype
he can say, my plays
are ~~the~~ autobiography of
tom horror. This is the simplest

Shakespeare" (91-28 Dec 17 1958). And so on for hundreds of ideas, scenarios, models, allusions, and analogies to Shakespeare.

In an unpublished draft introduction to *Another Bloody Page from Plutarch,* Watson notes that, "while writing the playscripts of this volume, I was trying, unsuccessfully, to incorporate Shakespeare's genetic word play into my texts" (95-115). Telling is *The Autobiography of Tom Horror,* the subtitle of *Plays at the Iron Bridge.* The subtitle puns on Macbeth's "Tomorrow and tomorrow and tomorrow / Creeps in its petty pace from day to day" (V.v.17–18). "The autobiography of tomorrow," Watson writes, "suggests the next day's looking back at the past; the autobiography of tom horror perceives this retrospection in the character (human) of someone involved and responsible and answerable" (95-117). This position, one Watson first enunciated in 1953 in a draft of a letter to accompany the manuscript of *Friday's Child,* was shaped by his reading of French playwright and philosopher Gabriel Marcel. Marcel cites "Macbeth's famous words" as "the literal truth" of nihilism (II.151), to be transcended by the intersubjectivity of someone "involved." In his draft letter, Watson had made a distinction between old modernity and "new modernism":

> There is going thru most of these poems a recognition that our modernity means that we are born very late in time — that good modernism means seeing modern man as the seed of the future, also as seeing that seed as the very late fruit of a very old tree. (91-6 July 29 1953)

This is the argument T.S. Eliot had made in "Tradition and the Individual Talent."

Left:
Wilfred Watson, aged about thirty-three, in Halifax in the Royal Canadian Naval Volunteer Reserve; J.D. Gallant, Halifax, photographer (95-24-3)

Right:
Wilfred Watson, graduate student at the University of Toronto; Ashley & Crippen, Toronto, photographer (95-24-02)

War, Doctoral Studies, Academia

War complicated everything. Upon completing his B.A. in 1943, Watson, who had considered registering as a conscientious objector (Flahiff, 56), enlisted in the Royal Canadian Naval Volunteer Reserve. For the next two years he worked below-decks as an electrician, first on patrols along the west coast of British Columbia and then stationed in Halifax. None of his wartime correspondence survives. But a notebook dated January 1945 begins with a list of five works, including material dating back to 1944. Three of these have been cut out. The remaining two are the earliest dated, although perhaps not the earliest, manuscripts in the Watson archive (91-01).

Demobilized, Watson headed to the University of Toronto's Ph.D. Program in English. His days as an artist-labourer were over; those as an artist-scholar had begun. In Toronto he taught first-year English, initially to students in the Ontario College of Pharmacy (95-115), then at University College. He turned his attention from Shakespeare to satire, working toward his 1951 Ph.D. thesis on "Sterne's Satire on Mechanism: A Study of Tristram Shandy." To judge by later notebook entries, his courses on Victorian Poetry and on Romanticism turned him into a relentless critic of both, as well as of Professor A.S.P. Woodhouse who taught them. He took courses on Spenser and Milton and found himself most at home in courses on Renaissance prose and on eighteenth-

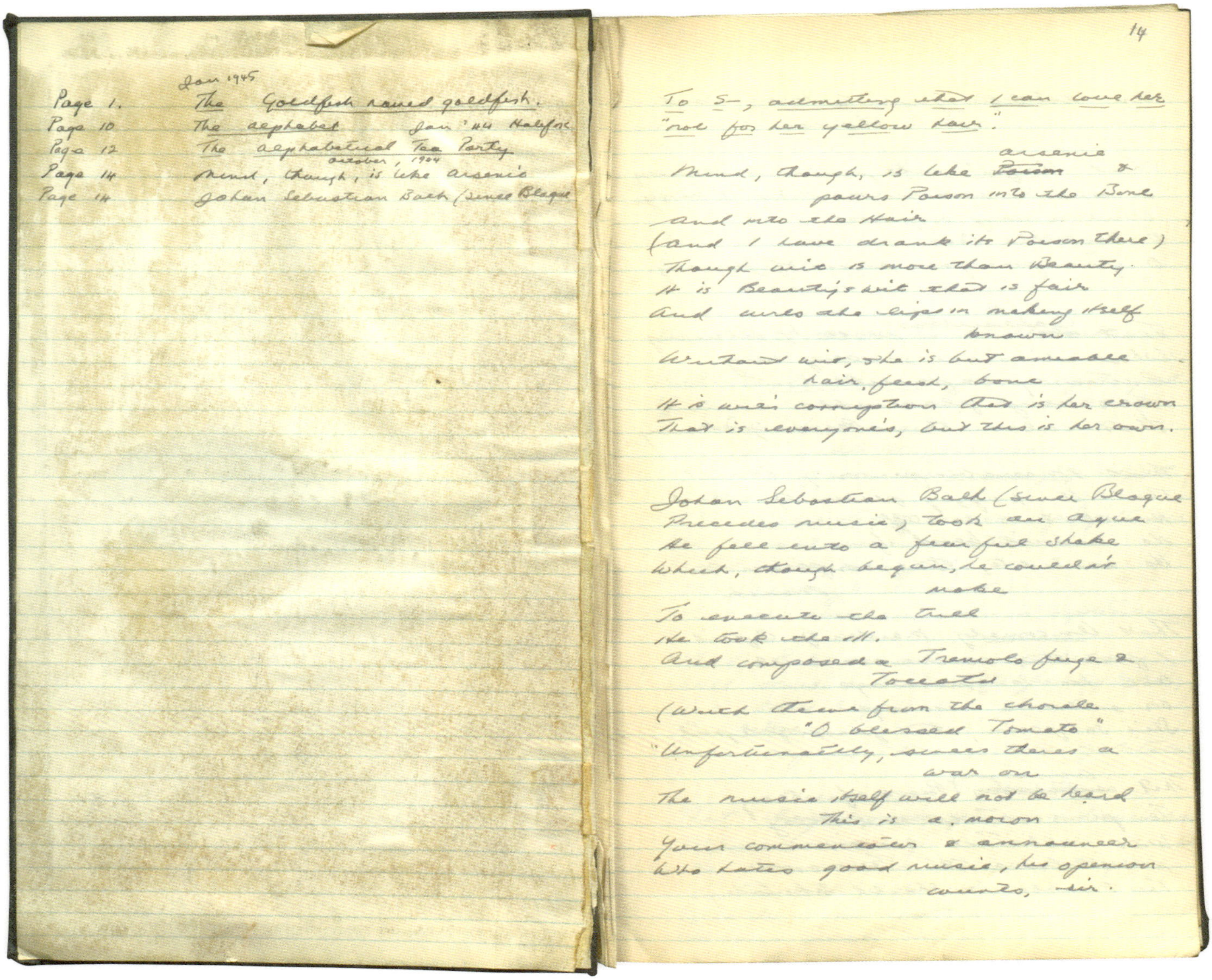

Jan 1945
Page 1. The Goldfish named goldfish.
Page 10 The alphabet Jan '44 Halifax
Page 12 The alphabetical Tea Party october, 1904
Page 14 Mind, though, is like arsenic
Page 14 Johan Sebastian Bach (since Blaque

14

To S—, admitting that I can love her
"not for her yellow hair."

Mind, though, is like arsenic ~~Poison~~ &
pours Poison into the Bone
and into the Hair
(and I have drank its Poison there)
Though wit is more than Beauty
It is Beauty's wit that is fair
And wets the lips in making itself
known
Without wit, she is but amiable
hair, flesh, bone
It is wit's corruption that is her crown
That is everyone's, but this is her own.

Johan Sebastian Bach (since Blaque
Precedes music) took an ague
He fell into a fearful shake
Which, though begun, he couldn't
make
To execute the trill
He took the ill.
And composed a Tremolo fuga &
Toccata
(With theme from the chorale
"O blessed Tomato"
"Unfortunately, since there's a
war on
The music itself will not be heard
This is a moron
Your commentator & announcer
Who hates good music, his sponsor
counts, sir.

Watson's earliest extant notebook, listing work from the war years and with a poem to Sheila Watson (91-01)

century writers. He rounded out his interests with a course on "17th-18th Century Political Thought" and another on "Descartes and the Cartesians." And he found a surprising artistic guide in the *Exeter Book*, in a course offered by Professor Shook in 1946–47. He would later tell Fred Flahiff that it was this course that taught him to write,[13] and in his notebooks for this year he drafts a series of "riddle" poems, using the Anglo-Saxon formula, "Saga hwaet ic hatte." The direct address of the riddle poems, which renders the speaking object immediately present, would become one of his chief dramatic aims.

6

Hctam

Peace was in the beautiful forest
Where I grew; many years I
flourished
There, in green sleep. My house
fell. Men bruised
Me. After I was dead, I found
A new life in a numerous family
In a smaller house. My brothers
And I were every one of us
hot-heads.
If my friend angers me, I flare
up, and my rage pleases him.
Sometimes what I leave
Devours that green forest. I pay
For my anger dearly with
My life. Say what I am.

An early "riddle" poem, 1947 (91-459)

To his study of Shakespeare, begun in grammar school, continued through his years of self-education and at UBC, and to his early self-directed reading of the Moderns, Watson on leaving the University of Toronto had added a deep understanding of satire and an equally deep admiration for the allegorical medieval morality play. He was ready to turn his hand to drama. The balance and counter-balance of autodidact and educated scholar would remain an integral part of his life and work. His reading retained the eclectic exploration of his early years as an autodidact: from his "escape" reading of anthropologists in his youth (91-17 July 16 1956) to existential and religious philosophers such as Sartre, Marcel, Maritain, and Weil; from books about the craft of playwriting to philosophers of aesthetics such as Bosanquet, Collingwood, and Read; from studies of the Greeks and Etruscans to historians of Modernist art; from Jung, Freud, Poulet, and parapsychologists to studies of the impact of technology (and this list takes us only up to 1957!). In his constant careful teasing out of meaning, language, and structure in Shakespeare, in his lifelong meditation on *Tristram Shandy*, in his frequent preoccupation with the classics of American literature, and in his erudite probing of McLuhan's ideas, he read, spoke, and wrote as a scholar.

A man who appears to have made friends easily, Watson remembered making none in Toronto (91-30 July 29 1959). Neither his background nor his temperament fitted him for the elitism he found in the University's graduate program. "Toronto kills the heart," he concluded at the end of four years (91-367). When Roy Daniells, Head of English at UBC, offered him a two-year contract as Special Lecturer (1949–1951), charged with teaching American literature, the Watsons returned to Vancouver. But when the "veteran-boom" ended, so did his job.

Lines: 'Toronto Lies at the Heart'

Toronto lies at the heart
A heaviness and an ache
As if the heart had shaped
Ugly and coarse as sin
Some thought it would unmake

A sun, a rain from heaven
Or hell may warm, may feed
A Florence or a Rome
Till from a sewer seed
Blows an immortal blossom

A marble house, or street
Ripe with the wealth
Of Peter's church.
And the mind magnificences, for
A thinking city

Can fill a man's heart full of thought,
And even rotten beauty
Can generate in decay
A living act. But here all glory

Dulls, stangles, dies the death.
Four years have taught
And in my heart I fear
Toronto kills the heart

"Toronto kills the heart"
(91-389)

80 words to a page
my sketchbook

The University of Alberta

In 1951, the year in which the Massey Royal Commission published its landmark report on national development in the arts and sciences, Watson successfully defended his Ph.D. thesis and took up a position at the recently created Calgary campus of the University of Alberta. There he taught American literature and first-year English, pursued his scholarship, and immediately became active in the University Drama Club, working on *Riders to the Sea* during his first year in Calgary and directing *A Phoenix Too Frequent*, in which he played Virilius, in his third. While at Calgary he also published the first two of seven "Whiskeyjack" columns he would write for *New Trail*, the magazine published by the Alumni Association of the University of Alberta. "Whiskeyjack" was an occasional column signed "G.P.", a.k.a. "Giles Patrick," the narrator of Watson's "The Double Life of Jeremy Patrick."[14] In his columns Watson good-humouredly satirized aspects of the University. His last two columns were exceptions. "Wingfeathers" praised F.M. Salter's *Medieval Drama in Chester* and Robert Orchard's Christmas 1954 direction of four medieval mystery plays. And "Whiskeyjack in Montmartre" recounted his attendance at Maurice Utrillo's funeral.

Calgary's status as a "branch" campus of the University of Alberta meant that Watson travelled to Edmonton each term for meetings with F.M. Salter, Chair of English, and for joint marking sessions. The Watsons spent at least one Christmas holiday and the summers in Edmonton; in 1954 Salter arranged for his transfer to the Edmonton campus. The English Department proved congenial for Salter warmly supported writers and creative writing courses, and Watson's colleagues included poets Eli Mandel and Ian Sowton, with whom he records many lively conversations, and novelists Henry Kreisel and, a few years later, Rudy Wiebe. In the late 1960s poets Doug Barbour and Stephen Scobie would join the department. "Henry and I have been projecting a writers' group," he wrote to Sheila Watson. "[W]hat I want is a small theatre group" (91-190a Nov 3 1956). Watson had just come back from a year of theatre-going in Paris where, attending performances by the Compagnie Madeleine Renaud-Jean-Louis Barrault, he had understood the advantages of having one's own troupe. "I wd. like it to swing toward a writers–actors club," he wrote of the proposal, "where we could work on drama, and so publish our own work. With it cd. go a teacher's group in Shakespeare" (91-17 Nov 3 1956).

A proposal for a "small theatre group" (91-17)

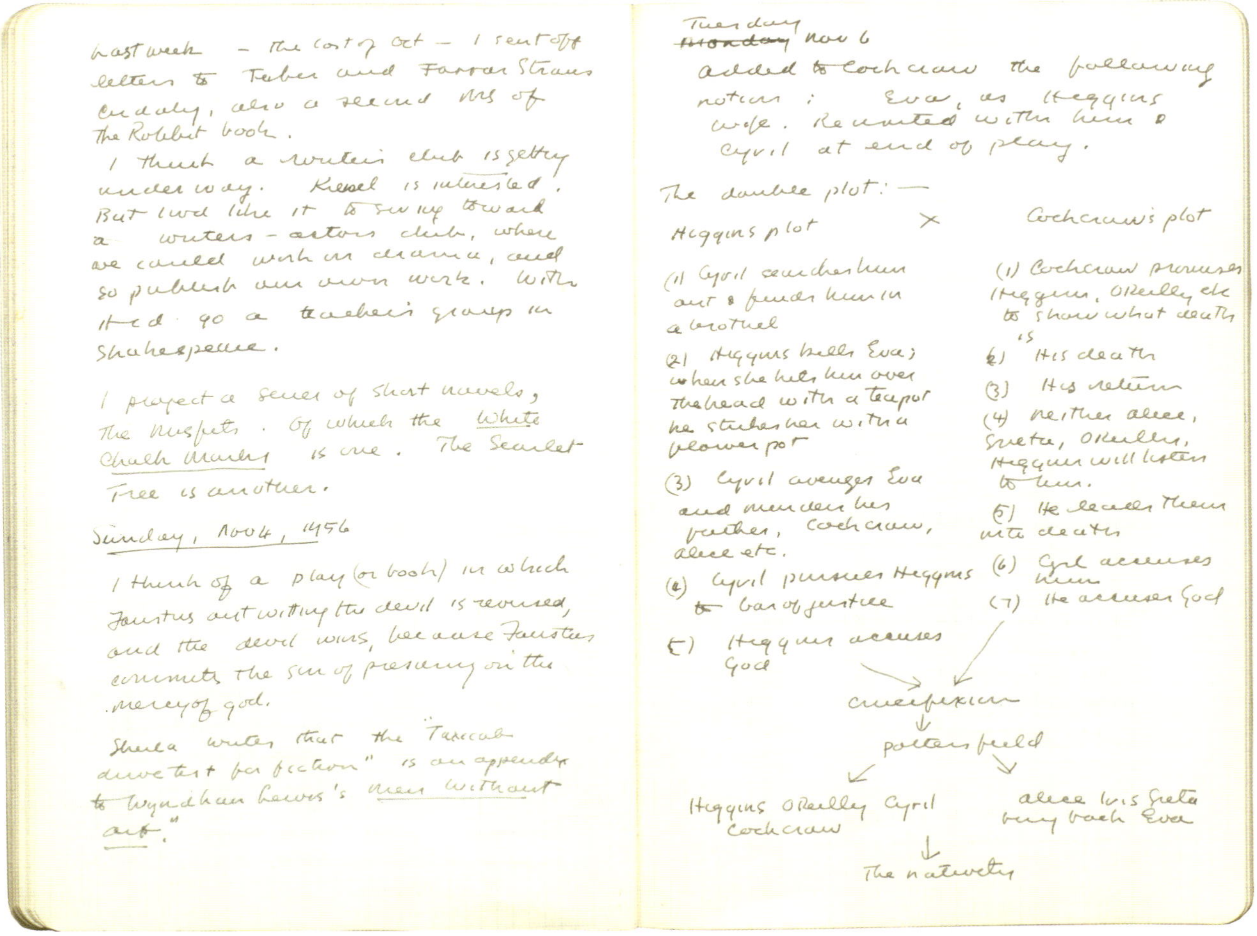

Edmonton's theatre scene, though largely amateur, was lively and venturesome. Watson participated in the annual Inter-Faculty One-Act Play Festival for which, in November 1957, he directed Ionesco's *The Bald Soprano*, winning the competition. In 1959, he directed his first produced play, "The Whatnot," "[f]rom a story by Gogol, freely domesticated and adapted by Wilfred Watson" (91-34) for the Festival. Though praised, it did not win. Robert Orchard, Professor of Drama, had established Studio Theatre in 1949; when he left for a position at CBC in 1955, Gordon Peacock took over the direction of the theatre and, a year later, established the Alumni Studio A Players.

Studio Theatre and Alumni Players performed a significant number of avant-garde European plays during these years: Pirandello, *Right You Are If You Think So* (1953); Giraudoux, *The Enchanted* (1954); no fewer than four Anouilh plays (1957 to 1958); Ionesco, *The Lesson* (1960); Brecht, *Galileo* (1961); Dürrenmatt, *The Visit* (1962). Not all, though, was avant-garde. We have noted Watson's "Whiskeyjack" praise for Robert Orchard's direction of four medieval morality plays, *From the Creation to the Nativity*, praise no doubt intensified by his own often stated desire to write a "morality play" in *Cockcrow and the Gulls*. When preparing *Plays at the Iron Bridge*, Watson summed up the importance to him of Gordon Peacock and Studio Theatre: "Edmonton Theatre [was] an experimental theatre, both in the sense of performing modern plays . . . and in the sense of working experimentally with theatre elements, like lighting, sound, space, etc. Part of Gordon Peacock's concept of the role of Studio Theatre was that it shd be a centre of activity for the whole community. Hence he gave encouragement & material assistance to splinter groups, like the Walterdale Playhouse, and the Yardbird Suite" (95-130), both of which would produce Watson.

Watson took his teaching seriously. He thought, for example, about a book on "the nature of literature and the teaching of E. L. to university freshman" and outlined its chapters (91-06 Dec 25 1954). His notebooks demonstrate an engagement with the American literature he had been hired to teach, and especially with Hawthorne's *The Scarlet Letter*, an adaptation of which he worked on at various times throughout the 1950s. Once in Edmonton, he began a prolonged, and sometimes contentious, process to have the Department approve a course in seventeenth-century literature that he offered for the first time in 1960–61. He also pushed for, and finally was given, the teaching

Patrons—Miss Maimie Simpson
Mr. Gordon Peacock
Elsie Park Gowan

The festival will be opened by the honorary p dent of the University of Alberta Drama Soc Elsie Park Gowan

Adjudicator—Mickey Macdonald
Well known Alberta actress and director, M Macdonald had an outstanding career on B way before returning to Edmonton and since time has distinguished herself here as a drar actress and director, as well as by playing lec roles in musical comedy. This is the second Mickey Macdonald has honored the Drama Sc by adjudicating this festival.

Trophies—Eva O. Howard Trophy awarded to club presenting the best one-act play. Pre winners:—
1955—Engineering
1956—Arts and Science
1957—Arts and Science
1958—Newman Club

The Drama Society will also present three vidual trophies, the recipients of which are to the discrimination of the adjudicator. may be presented for special merit in any pha theatrical work.

STUDIO THEATRE, University of Alberta
presents
THE ALUMNI PLAYERS' PRODUCTION
of
TIME REMEMBERED
by Jean Anouilh
December 9, 10, 11, 12
at 8:30 sharp
Phone GE 3-3265 for Reservations
Box Office—Main Lobby, Education Buildin
82 Avenue and 112 Street
10:00 a.m. to 5:00 p.m. from November 2
Tickets $1.00 and $1.50
STUDENT PERFORMANCE
Tuesday, December 8th, Special Price 75c

MONDAY, NOVEMBER 23
8:30 p.m.

NURSES (MACLEOD CLUB)

LADIES ALONE

Florence Ryerson and Colin Clements

Norah	Leslie Beattie
Peggy	Lynne Crowsley
Marge	Stella McKibbon

Time—an early spring evening.
Place—a small apartment

Director—Ansley Day
Assistant Director—Elisabeth Thiel
Costumes—Helen Cameron
Sets and Properties—Lorna Hughes

AGRICULTURE

IN THE ZONE

Eugene O'Neil

Ivan	Leighton Mellemstrand
Swanson	Jim Rae
Scotty	Ron Gordon
Smitty	Al Stewart
Davis	Robert Ewashen
Driscoll	George Rife
Cocky	Frank Fretwell
Jack	Murray Turnbull

Time—An early morning in 1940.
Place—The forecastle of the S.S. Glencairn, a tramp steamer plying the Atlantic with a cargo of ammunition.

Director—Garry Mitchell
Properties—Al Stewart

UNIVERSITY OF ALBERTA DRAMA SOCIETY

presents

THE SHEWING-UP OF BLANCO POSNET

by

George Bernard Shaw

CAST

Babsy	Regine Van Hyfte
Lottee	Elsie Lobur
Hannah	Divana Schumacher
Jessie	Barbara Taylor
Emma	Elke Egge
Elder Daniels	Richard Wray
Blanco Posnet	Garry Mitchell
Strapper Kemp	Martin Kochuk
Feemy	Maureen Murphy
Sheriff Kemp	Larry Ewashen
The Foreman	George Lane
Nestor	Harold Dootson
Waggoner Jo	Don Wells
The Heavenly Woman	Rosalind Bull
The Boys	Simon Peers, Duncan Marshall, Willis Brink, Oliver Weisbeck, John Elliot, Peter Kirchmeir, Don Robertson, Scott Klipper, Bob Ewashen, Roy Halvstrom, Clint Sopchyshyn, Ken Wernka

Director—Michael Porsca
Production and Stage Manager—Ken Westerlund
Stage Director—Don Wells
Costume Designing—Divana Schumacher and Merrillee Firth
Properties—Donna Gale
Prompter—Helen Anderson
Technical—Bob Enders
Stage Crew—Bob Paston and Gary Wilson

Setting—A town in the American West.
Time—1850's.

This presentation, the winner of the Edmonton Drama League Regional One-Act Festival, is not for competition.

TUESDAY, NOVEMBER 24
8:30 p.m.

ARTS AND SCIENCE (A.S.U.S.)

THE WHATNOT

From a story by Nicolai Gogol. Freely domesticated and adapted for the stage by Dr. Wilfred Watson

Announcer	Vivienne Rowley
George Plumtree	Bob Mumford
Bob Green	Arthur Robinson
Mary Green	Ann Hardy
Geoffrey Brown	Drake Hocking
Stephanie Brown	Nola Hague
Ardrienne Goolich	Joan Caldwell
Mrs. Bollingen-Ford-Guggenheim	Rondo Wood

Time—A cool September day.

Director—Kay Martin
Advisor—Dr. W. Watson
Prompter—Dr. White

Program of the Inter-Faculty One-Act Play Festival, Nov 1959, including "The Whatnot" (91-34)

of Shakespeare. He advocated strongly for a course in Canadian literature, although in its early years he was reluctant to teach it. His last graduate course, in 1975–76, was a seminar on Canadian literature of the 1960s. And he supervised many graduate students.

During the twenty-five years that Watson taught in Edmonton, universities increasingly focused on research and Watson turned repeatedly to plans for a book on *Tristram Shandy*, and just as often abandoned them in favor of a novel or a play. He gave a paper, "Interstructuralization in Drama and the Other Arts," at the Humanities Association in 1961, planned an unwritten book on what he called "genetic" or "structural" wordplay in Shakespeare, and published a paper on the subject. In 1956 he proposed to Macmillan a "Viking Portable Canadian Reader" (95-190a WW to SW Nov 3 [1956]), an anthology he privately titled "The Bleak Pastoral." After some back and forth, he signed a contract with Roy Daniells as co-editor (95-194, WW to SW Nov 7 [1957]). Although the two were good friends who relished each other's conversation and wit, the collaboration was potentially fraught given that only a month before he had characterized Daniell's essay on Canadian literature in *The Culture of*

Thursday

Dear Swp

again, our bitter weather has gentled into a thaw. Tonight a very lovely evening. I wonder how the thesis is boiling? Sir, I turn the fowl on a spit. But it's still crowing? Which, Sir, proves my point: it crows in emblems, Sir.

I have had a letter from Roy D. on my conscience some few days – with respect – the letter – to the anthology. Finally, last night I hit on a solution. I think of a 'diagnostic' anthology including second-rate stuff but not excluding first-rate work, if any. With commentaries, for and against, by me & Roy.

"Trueman" and "Freeman"
(95-228 WW to SW Feb 1957)

Contemporary Canada as "a very bad piece of work, full of prejudice, lack of balance often for the right reasons" (SW-514 WW to SW Oct 3 [1957]). Daniells suggested casting the anthology as a dialogue between Trueman (himself), who would present the orthodoxies of literary nationalism in Canada, and Freeman (Watson), who would respond to them (95-198 WW to SW May 31 1958).[15] The two men met most enjoyably a number of times to discuss the project, but it came to naught. Both were busy with other work: Daniells with his own scholarship and poetry and his work as Head of

This was his excellent idea — The notion we might make a point of difference of opinion. I feel we could call the book, The Bleak Pastoral or, alternatively, The Nurseries of Wilderness (a phrase from Dylan Thomas). With our dialectic, we cd. really be tough on our authors — yet there might be zest in it — and — at any rate it wd. stir up interest. We should also be able to include the standard anthology stuff. What do you think? Have you any liking for either of the titles, or can you think of a better?

I send you on the Alec Hope letter. I'd like it back when you've read it — to answer.

English at UBC; Watson with *Cockcrow and the Gulls*, *The Trial of Corporal Adam*, the unpublished poetry collection "The Scaffold of Joy," his occasional directing, his essay on "Instructuralization." In the summer of 1961, three years after their contract specified delivery of the manuscript, Daniells wrote to Macmillan to abort the project.

The anthology and the never-to-be-completed books on Sterne and on Shakespeare offer indices of Watson's changing relation to the English Department in the 1960s and 1970s. At a time of increasing research specialization, Watson quietly — sometimes not so quietly — insisted on remaining a generalist; in the face of increasing Canadian nationalism, he resisted an idea of national "identity" constructed around the content of a literary work or its author's citizenship. By the mid-1940s he had already been writing fiction and plays as well as poetry, and his notebooks reveal that he often developed an idea in several genres. He thought of himself as a writer and an artist before he thought of himself as a scholar, and he thought of himself as a writer and an artist before he thought of himself specifically as a playwright or a poet.

After he returned from Paris in 1956, he sought out a creative community that went well beyond the Department of English, working with professors Gordon Peacock and Thomas Peacocke in the Drama Division and serving as a member of the Division's committee to establish a program in playwriting; "I'd ultimately like to teach playwriting, possibly in the Dept of Drama," he wrote Sheila Watson, who was at the University of Toronto pursuing her Ph.D. (SW-514[5] Feb 16 [1958]). He collaborated with painter and set designer Norman Yates from the Department of Art and Design, whom he several times credited with teaching him about visual space and enabling him to go beyond Marshall McLuhan's category of the visual. In Edmonton, he worked with the Students' Union to produce his "Up Against the Wall, Oedipus"; he collaborated with Walterdale Playhouse and the Yardbird Suite; and, in the early 1980s, he prepared a script including work from *The Sorrowful Canadians* and *I Begin with Counting* for performance by Donna Gruhlke and Raymon Montalbetti. Watson found his community in Edmonton's theatre scene first, in the English Department second.

"The Trial," an early poem on a recurring theme of the injustice of justice (91-459)

The Trial

One day, to Ruth, for judgment came
Two lawyers, hearing of her fame —
Her justice, giving each his due —
Her learning large, but able, too —
Her mercy, kind as Portia's —
Her wisdom — turn we to the Cause:—
The cause, a murder or a rape —
No matter, 'twas of such a shape —
That nice discretion must decide
The guilt of him whose case is tried;
A cause made difficult & fine
By two shrewd lawyers, who to dine
Must make clear matters somewhat subtle,
With sharp rejoinder & rebuttal.

Her wig and gown of office donned, her
Face of office, grave to ponder;

The case is heard; first lawyer Styles
Steps forward with a gracious smile.

His dress is decorous & neat;
His manner eloquent & discreet.
His wig of lambswool, finely curled;
His coat, that of a man of the world;
His gestures spoke, his flashing eye —
O, how cd such an aspect lie?
Could one who helped himself to snuff
So delicately, stoop to bluff?
Could such a nostril, such a nose
T'avoid ~~miasma~~ an odour, scent the rose,
Not by a correlated sense,
Sniff out the fact from the pretence?

Could such discernment in address
Stoop from itself, half-truth to express,
To shift a meaning, hint a lie,
Or a half-prejudice imply?
Could such discretion in a glove
Not be unmatched, in Things above?

In one so dressed, twere almost spite
To add an argument of right;

Below:
"Poems, 1936/1985," draft outline (not used) for *Poems: Collected/Unpublished/New* (95-112)

Early Poetry: The Thinking Heart

Poems, 1936/1985

I the poem as aboriginal self
II the poem as gender or not-self
III the poem as constructed or extended self
IV the poem as experimental self
V the poem as ritual self

Watson's papers from the time he was preparing his *Poems: Collected/Unpublished/New* include a draft subtitle, "Poems, 1936/1985" (95-112). Since he does not appear to have culled his papers after preparing the manuscript of *Poems*, this tantalizing scrap suggests that the archive may hold some poems dating from his mid-twenties. If so, they are in the manuscripts titled "Canvasses Point Grey." One of its poems, dedicated to "R[oy] D[aniells]," who had made possible his return to Vancouver, implies that Watson had not found his years in Toronto conducive to poetry and that his homecoming to Vancouver proved a release: "After four years of prose, there came / A year of poetry, a year of flame"; "the eye comes home" and the "heart find[s] herself at last withdrawn / Across her threshold home again" (91-384). Watson almost certainly assembled "Canvasses Point Grey" during his second year at UBC in 1950–51. We do not know whether he submitted it to a publisher. Nor can we be sure of the entire contents of the original collection, since folders with this title mix poems we do know to have belonged to it with later poems (see 91-389 and 91-369).

Our clearest guide to Watson's earliest poetry is "The Dark Village and Other Poems," a collection he assembled in late 1951 (91-189 SW to WW Dec 9 1951). The title of "Prolusions" given to its first poems, as well as their style and content, suggests that they are among his earliest extant writing. Although their syntax is occasionally convoluted and their diction sometimes archaic, they display an easy facility with conventional and slant rhyme, regular and sprung rhythm, and traditional verse forms. They are all structured around or towards a question, or conceit, or idea, such as that of the poem that opens this section (and will close *Friday's Child*) that "Letters are hearses and this one brings / My dead thoughts, relics, not living things" (91-384; *Friday's Child*, 56). The second section, "Canvasses Point Grey," is for the most part *plein air* "painting" in poetry and often involves an epiphany or a reversal. Typical is "Morning, November 1949, West Point Grey":

> Pale primrose was that dawn and the sky a-flower
> With world's beauty, and the earth nymphs and the angels
> Of heaven rejoicing in that marrying hour:
> . . . Some fate had waked me all this to behold,
> These incongruous nuptials. . . .
> I stand and watch on feet of numbness; wayward the day
> A monstrous offspring and a late unclasping. (91-384)

A "Good Friday" poem from "The Dark Village" (91-384)

The third section, "The Dark Village," from which the collection takes its title, turns from nature to man, and man's injustice to man. The tower, the scaffold, and the prison figure largely as the latter two would throughout his *oeuvre.* Watson rewrites myths for modern times, one of which, "Tarquin," he retained for *Friday's Child.* And in "The Dark Village" we have the first of what will be a series of "Good Friday" poems, exploring the symbolism of the Crucifixion (91-384). A fourth section, "For Gillian," collected some of the "Saga hwaet ic hatte" riddles he had written in 1947; he thought well enough of them to include three in his 1986 *Poems.*

"The Queen of Tarts," the fifth section, enunciated an important principle underpinning all of Watson's poetry and drama from this point forward: that we cannot know the spirit except as it is incarnated. He subtitled the section "ballads celebrating the soul's love for the body" and opened it with "The Soul's Epithalamium; for its bride, the body," which he wisely retitled "O My Poor Darling" when he published it in *Friday's Child*. The later collection also included one of the three "Queen of Tarts" poems from "The Dark Village." The rhythms of these poems are looser and more passionate, the diction more colloquial, earthier, than that of previous sections. One hears echoes of W.B. Yeats in his "Crazy Jane" poems; one also hears Watson beginning to find a way to speak through a persona. The volume concluded with "Other Poems" that didn't fit under the stylistic or thematic groupings of the previous five sections. These included two that found their way into *Friday's Child*: "Emily Carr" and "To the Shadbolts, with Six Quinces from Duncan." Taken as a whole — in its evidence of influence, in its experiments, in its many voices, in its rhythms, diction, imagery, and emergent symbols — the proposed collection documents Watson's extensive apprenticeship to poetry.

We do not know whether he submitted "The Dark Village" to a publisher and met with chastening rejection, whether he shared it only with fellow poets for comment, or whether he sat on it and reconsidered. By June 1952, however, a month in which he was full

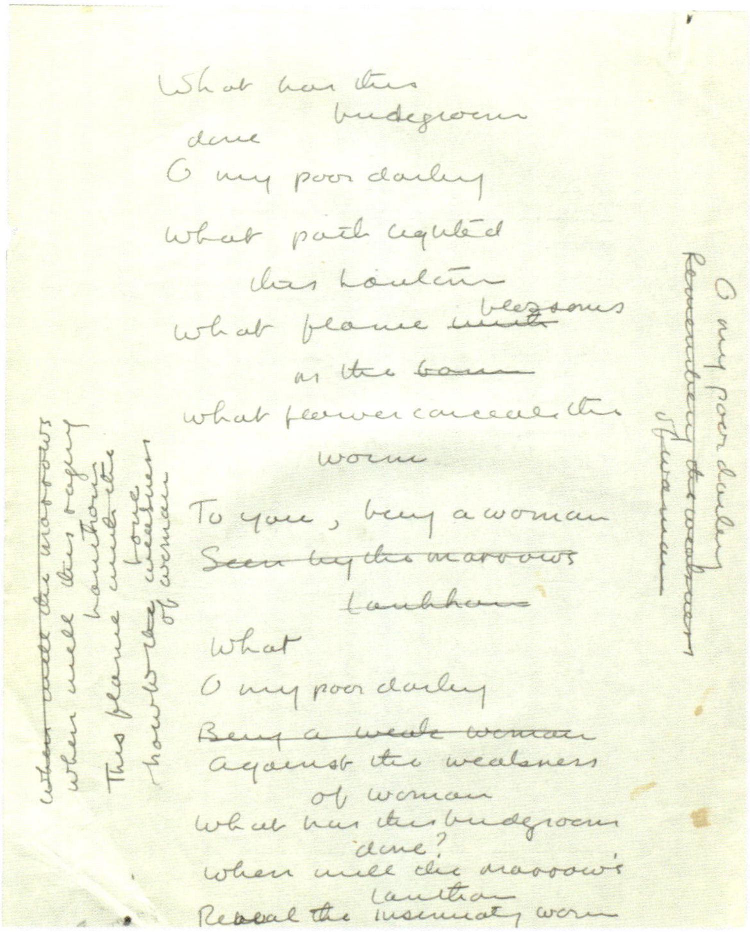

Two early drafts of lines from "O My Poor Darling" (91-369)

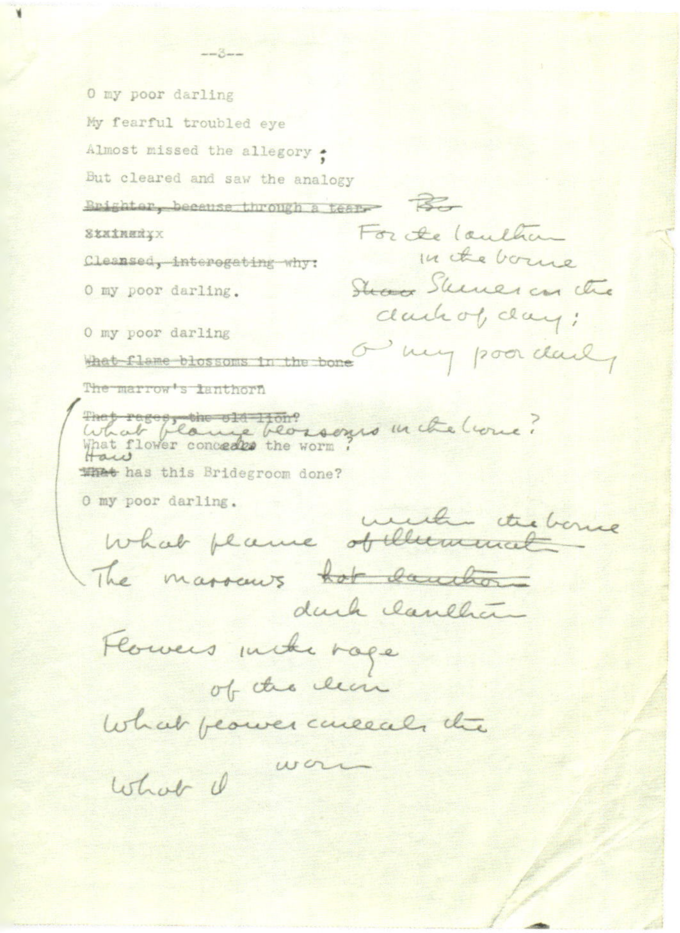

To S.....

Ask me not why your tenderness of ways
Has gentled me, for I could find you reason;
So blooms the flower according to the sun
And to the sun turns her enchanted face
Though yet her blossoming were an act of
grace;
I could name your beauty an oblivion
Wherein to sink the world's blemish and drown
My own defect in deep forgetfulness--
I could name a hundred hundred things
That move me to you on an angel's wings;
There are the reasons of a loving heart
But all these reasons from this love do
start;
Rather a music in my being springs
Which I made not although I know the
part.

of new ideas for poems, he wanted to make his syntax and metrics easier for the contemporary ear. He noted that he had "experimented" with Marlowe's line only to "sense that the over-subtle line defeats most readers. Witness Donne's, or Wyatt's wrenched metres. My tendency is to follow Donne or Wyatt. But I shall try for a more regular line, still keeping the subtlety within the regularity" (91-6 June [actually July] 30 1952).

By the end of the following summer, he had prepared the submission of his work to a number of poetry magazines only to have it, as we have already noted, universally rejected. And he had prepared a new manuscript, "Friday's Child" (91-367 draft letter to Ann Taylor Aug 3 1953). He drafted a description of its poems as falling "neatly into three groups. The first, Jocasta and other poems are recreations of myth with modern application somewhat in the manner of Sartre and Anouilh and the French." The second section was

Above:
"My tendency is to follow Donne or Wyatt": a poem written to Sheila Watson (91-456)

815, 16th Avenue West,
Calgary, Alberta.

August 3, 1953

Ann Taylor, Editor,
McClelland and Stewart,
Toronto, Ontario.

Dear Miss Taylor,

I am sending you on a manuscript of FRIDAY'S CHILD in hope you will be able to consider it for publication. Some of these poems have been published ~~fairly~~ recently in magazine form: "Emily Carr", "Orpheus and Eurydice", "The Queen of Tarts", "To the Shadbolts with Six Quinces from Duncan", and "Let These Trumpets Tongued with Dust". The others, with an exception or two, date within the past eighteen months.

Perhaps I should say something ~~to explain~~ about the title. What has preoccupied me ~~in the past while~~ has been a search for the conditions of progress in a time when the word itself is tarnished badly. The idea behind these poems is the recognition that, if modern man is the seed of the future, he is also the fruit of a very old tree. This idea has its culmination in "Love Song for Friday's Child". So it seemed right to call the whole collection FRIDAY'S CHILD. We are, as it were, born late in the week, and these are poems of that fact.

Yours sincerely,

Wilfred Watson

I told Roy Daniells I was keeping my promise to make this collection and send it on to you. He said (I suppose he was pulling my leg) he would like to be your reader.

Right:
Draft letter to Ann Taylor, McClelland and Stewart, to accompany submission of *Friday's Child* (91-367)

Contents

Invocation : Appear, O Mother

Jocasta and Other Poems

Jocasta
Orpheus and Eurydice I
Orpheus and Eurydice II
Pasiphae
Proserpina I : "The Flower"
Proserpina II : "The Marriage with Death"
Et Incarnatus Est

An Admiration for Dylan Thomas and other poems

Kwakiutl Poles
Emily Carr
An Admiration for Dylan Thomas
To the Sahdbolts with Six Quinces from Duncan
Lines on Rembrandt's "Bathsheba"
Verse Letter to Dorothy Bazett
To the Haleys, who sent Dahlias
Lines: There is a babe in an old man growing
Lines: He seemed a Shade Removed
The Queen of Tarts
OaMy Poor Darling
Lines: Let No Other Friend Know Me
And Should she Ask
Lines: I Praise God's Mankind in an Old Woman

Friday's Child and Other Poems

A Valediction for the End of the Year
In the Cemetery of the Sun
Love Song for Friday's Child

Epilogue: For Anne, Who Brought Tulips

Table of Contents for the 1953 version of *Friday's Child* (91-369)

the poems of "An Admiration for Dylan Thomas and other poems." "The final group, Good Friday's Child," he wrote, "is very recent, and [the] result of a single inspiration" (*Ibid*). The "Table of Contents" reveals Watson severely culling his selection: where "The Dark Village" had included approximately one hundred poems, this version of "Friday's Child" included only twenty-six (91-369). Among those jettisoned were all of the "Canvasses, Point Grey" poems. Within months, he returned to the collection, removing a further eleven poems from it, and adding sixteen, including new poems and "Tarquin" from "The Dark Village." This is this manuscript Sheila Watson sent to T.S. Eliot.

If T.S. Eliot thought *Friday's Child* the first real poetry written in Canada (SW-05 May 9 1956), reviewers were near unanimous in noting the influence of Dylan Thomas, the most appreciative of them describing the collection as "the first good volume to be published in England which could not have been written if Thomas had not

April 29. I have some time
being thinking of a Religio
like Browne's (and even
a commentary on Browne's)
a sort of Handbook not
to give Truth, but to suggest
its topics, some of its topics.
I wd. like to see what
Christianity says to the
imperfect man, the man
cast off by the churches.
Not to gainsay the churches,
but rather to see if there is
a complement to their Truth.

I thought how philosophy
begins with our recognition
we can think of things;
and that poetry begins when
we think of our feelings.
Some poetry does little more
than describe feelings. But
the greatest poetry invokes
and celebrates emotion
intellectualized and patterned
about some centre.

April 30 I drove down to
Calgary, and put Poto
in with Miss Hammond.
I don't understand the
arrangement, so possibly
it will work. I then
drove back.
Sheila told Salter (so she
admits) that she wants
no more experience, that is,
to be a writer. I understand
what she feels — that what
is needed is a surcease
of life, in order that
contemplation may have
a little peace.

"Poetry begins when we think of our feelings"; journal entry April 29 1955 (91-09)

written . . . fruitfully" (Anon.). Watson's notebooks show him defining his own poetics both in relation to and against Dylan Thomas and by comparison with English poet Vernon Watkins, whose *Death Bell and Other Poems* the Watsons read with admiration in the spring of 1955. On the same day that Faber and Faber sent Watson a contract (91-367 P.F. du Sautoy to WW Jan 25 1955), he contextualized "A Contempt for Dylan Thomas," acknowledging that he "had learned much from his orchestration of emotion," but also judging that "his images . . . do not penetrate into the inner meaning of things, or human nature." For Watson, the poet must feel "in order to understand, not to revel in feeling. But the highest poetry pertains to the seeing and thinking heart" (91-6 Jan 25 1955 draft letter to R[odney] P[oisson]). In April, when he read Watkins with admiration, Watson described Thomas's verse as "'images and cry.' All else he abdicates — the thinking heart I do not find in Thomas. . . . of the rocky coast of the heart he tells us little and nothing of the desert of the mind" (91-9 Mar 30 1955).

The ideal of poetry as the "thinking heart" owes something to Watson's admiration for the Metaphysical poets. Some years later, preparing for his course on seventeenth-century poetry, he cited approvingly Odette de Mourgue's comments about the "'perfect poise'" between "'intellectual ratiocination'" and "'passionate feeling'" in the Metaphysical poets, and applied them to himself: "To me, . . . the poet recognizes two absolutely antithetic neighbours in the universe, and his reconciliation is the truth that the universe holds both . . . what is balanced is a force and its opposite, so that both are seen in a conflict of extreme drama" (91-37 May 22 1960).

The conception of poetry as the work of the "seeing and thinking heart" as well as Watson's analysis and reconsideration of *Friday's Child,* even as it was in press, owed a great deal to his reading, in late 1953, of Gabriel Marcel's *Mystery of Being*, a work he spent many years thinking through. Marcel stood with other existentialists in his argument that consciousness is incarnated and that we live in a "broken world" in which scientific positivism, bureaucracy, and despotic governments degrade imagination, reflection, and creativity. Both recognitions are core to Watson's work. Marcel countered what he understood as the closed and abstract "primary reflection" of science and "technique" by a "secondary reflection" open to intersubjectivity, that is, to a yearning to transcend the ego and become fully "present" to oneself and to others. Here he parted ways with existentialists such as Sartre; this intersubjectivity, he argued, is a necessary condition of creativity and it leads us to "mystery," to intersubjectivity with God. Watson's notebooks during the 1950s are full of meditations and ideas derived from Marcel. Although the philosopher's influence on the Canadian playwright's work deserves careful study, here, a sort of "credo" Watson wrote late in the composition of *Cockcrow and the Gulls* must stand as an index of the importance to his "generation" of Marcel's existentialism:

> Our first article of belief is: That there is no religious revelation, except through art. (2) Art is not a vehicle, but a "body" of religious truth.
>
> Behind this belief is an unexpressed dogma, that man as a spirit is limited and defined by a body, and that this body is essential to him (cf. the dogma of the resurrection of the body.)
>
> Hence our interest in the existential. Existentialism is the philosophy of spirits existing in bodies . . . existential political philosophy is the philosophy of men in state. Etc. The aim of the state, ultimately is to produce art.

Hence our interest in death.
Hence our dissatisfaction with science. . . .
The function of a state, is to produce, protect, and to express itself in its artists. . . . No civilization is of any moment, except in its art. In a sense, the state which has no art, has no existence. That is why Canada now is chafing about its lack of art. Canada doesn't exist.

This is a "religion for art's sake" view? Of course.

One doesn't invent a religion. One finds out what one's religion is. (91-33 Feb 13 1960)

Table of Contents for the unpublished collection "Scaffold of Joy" (91-387)

Although Marcel's ideas became central to Watson's own understanding of himself as an artist, they initially proved difficult to realize with clarity and weighed down his drafts for the play *Cockcrow and the Gulls* and for the poetry written, in the years immediately following *Friday's Child*, for a collection he titled "Scaffold of Joy."

Several of the poems in that collection, such as "The Blue-Eyed Tree"(91-446), "A Canticle of Children" (91-456), and "Ballad of Joy" (91-371), attempt to work out an allegory of the Crucifixion, in terms not only of Marcel but of Watson's own concept of the Crucifixion as re-enacted in every gift of one to another. One, "Scaffold of Children," attempts a verse dialogue on the subject, with a sure-to-fail cast that includes Adam and Eve, John the Baptist and Mary Magdalene, Hester Prynne and Dimmesdale (91-456). The poetry of 1956 to 1958 was further complicated by Watson's conception of it as a "gift," in Marcel's sense, to a young woman, Joyce Wontner, with whom he had fallen in love in 1952. She ended the relationship in August 1956, but he would "dedicate" — or give — himself and his work to her until at least 1960.[16] In at least one of the poems, "This City" (91-446), Watson apostrophized her. The punning title of the collection references both her name and Marcel's conviction that "when we are in the presence of God," "the last word must be with love and joy" (II.177) for "joy is an exaltation" (II.119). The private and the public allegory proved impossible to bring intelligibly together.

Table of contents

Facing page:
A page from the poem "Ballad of Joy" (91-371)

O wool-wound lamb my joy

What so you know of the warm of joy, wool-wound lamb?
What do you know of the joy of warm, my lamb?
I lilt on fields of paradise
And I am light to need the warm of wool

O soft pearl my joy

What do you know of the several tears of joy, soft pearl?
What do you know of the joy of tears, my pearl?
I saw loss in the fisherman's eyes
And I was soon to give myself to the nets

O green tree my joy

What do you know of the living green, green tree?
What do you know of the passion of green, my tree?
I held love up in my bent arms
And I was weak to cry the hangman's nail

O lord Christ my joy

What so you know of the joy of love, lord Christ?
What do you know of the heart of joy, my Christ?
For love I took on human flesh
But I was woe to leave my mother's arms

-/-

Corporal lance-jack lop-eared private. The drab
cow
And the grey coyote are brighter pellaged by far than
they,
The drab fellows who make this city its clothes
Who cook its meats and bake its cakes and loaves
Who tread its sheets and live its lives --
Brighter by far the ordinary sparrows
Who live by fraud against the scarlet berry

**

The bread goes wrong. The wheat in the beginning
grows well
Does well. But something in the miller or in the
mill
Defeats the germ. Or in the baker, or in the oven
In the yeast perhaps or in the shortening
Something in the ingredient or in the ingredience
Destroys the flavour of the sun. The bread goes
wrong
The cafes are as shabby and drear as brothels
The meals they serve lack soul and wine
God would be ashamed to be turned into this food
Into this bread and drink. The bread goes wrong
O Joyce, who thought man's food celebrates his soul
O joyce, this city is damned in its bread and ale
O Joyce, this mercenary bread declares its miserable
soul

***

Coin is the lieutenant-governor. Coin the mayor
Coin is the prime minister and his prayer
Coin is the executive and legislature
Coin is the magistracy and the law
Coin is the judge fining the robber
Coin is the RCMP redbreasting the bootlegger in his
bottle
Coin is the constable to constable the whore in her
brothel
Coin is the school-teacher saying her classes
Coin is the Minister of Education smiling at the
masses
Coin is the prim professor and coin his philosophy
Coin is the _summum bonum_ of the university
Coin is the doctor. Coin the cancer
Coin is the surgeon weeping behind his scalpel
Coin is the matron padlocking her hospital
Coin is the druggist. Coin his drug
Coin is the undertaker and sings hymns in the morgue
Coin is the ball-player and coin his sport
Coin is the artist and coin his art
Coin is the poet pulling on his phrases
Coin is the bridegroom taking off his trousers
Coin the bride's kiss --
Coin is the architect. Coin made this city to be
what it is

****

Passages from the central sections of "This City," written in late 1956 (91-446)

In the fall of 1956 Watson found himself alone and lonely in Edmonton; he and Sheila had separated,[17] and Joyce had held out for a marriage that divorce law of the time did not allow him to offer. His distress is perhaps reflected in poems such as "The Blue-Eyed Tree," "Lines at the Full of the Moon," or "This City" (91-446), or in lines such as these in which the imagery is noticeably darker than that of *Friday's Child*:

> As I was walking all alone
> I heard ten corbies making moan
> The one unto the other say,
> What ballad s[h]all we twa
> Peck the eyes out of today? ("The Ballad of Faustus" 91-387)

Despite his dark mood and his complex allegorical aims, Watson did realize poetic advances in this collection. He employed a looser, more variable line, often unrhymed, that more closely approximates the colloquial speech he hoped to achieve in the verse of *Cockcrow and the Gulls*, the play he was also writing at this time. This is particularly evident in a poem such as "The Blackberry Pickers."[18] Within the structure of the "requiem" of "A Lullaby for Falstaff," he presented the fat knight's death as a versified set of stage directions for a "dumbshow," taking a significant step towards dramatizing his verse (91-368). We also see him using choruses in ways that prefigure his plays and poetry of the 1960s.

Watson sent "Scaffold of Joy" to Faber and Faber, where it was rejected within the month (SW-9 June 6 1958; 91-25 July 4 1958). Indeed, despite the coup of *Friday's Child* and its Governor General's Award, he faced continued rejection. *The London Magazine* and *New World Writing* both turned back poems he sent them in 1955–56. Faber and Faber wanted revisions, which he never completed, to his novel "The Rabbit's Paw" (95-344 Montieth to WW Nov 26 1956). Paul Wright at CBC turned back two short stories (91-28 Jan 7 1958). Coach House Press rejected *Cockcrow and the Gulls* (91-33 Nov 28 1959) and, though Watson had hopes that Robert Corrigan would include it in a collection of new American plays, this did not happen. "I have been on the whole wonderfully unsuccessful in life, with respect to what I've tried to do," Watson wrote with some bravado. "With it all comes a single blessing: I have only really thought that the struggle with the medium mattered. Once I've written a poem, I don't care if I publish it. . . . The majority of modern poets follow the example of the greatest living poet, T.S. Eliot, and publish their own work" (91-30 July 29 1959).

Facing page: Watson "speaks" to Eliot about the rejection of "Scaffold of Joy" and about what he has learned from reading Wyndham Lewis; journal entry Aug 13 1958 (91-25)

Which is what he would, in effect, do during the 1960s and 1970s. While both *Canadian Literature* and *Prism* proved receptive to the publication of an occasional poem from the late '50s and early '60s, Watson's next collection, *The Sorrowful*

spatially – that is,
philosophically, not
picturesquely, considered,
directions have no meaning
without something to give
them meaning. It
is the baby which gives
significance to the
cradle, the mother &
father.

Is this not typical of Dylan
Thomas's as well as
Jamie Reaney's imagery:
it is picturesque, not
significant, not spatial?

Swift's 'kissing the horse's
hoof' is a significant
spatial image.

= Spatial poems are not
common in English.

= I've been asking certain
questions. I've just been
reading a very fine
thesis, about Melville,
by a student of mine.
When presented, the thesis
got little acclaim – not
what it shd have got –
because the assigned
readers detected a
hastiness in the writing,
which (as I'd asked for
extensive revisions just
before the deadline) was in
fact there. I think you &
Faber have detected an
uneveness in these
lost poems – and I concur.

But – now – I think
I have passed from
them, as transition, to the
achievement I want. The
touch came from a
study of Wyndham Lewis.
The key is 'space' –
dramatic or significant
space – and I think
you have thought enough
about 'space' / 'time' to
see the possibility of a
poetry in which sculptor's
space is applied to imagery.
I think of the significance
of space between horse &
rider, actor and actor,
the lover and his beloved,

man and God. All the
intimations of the poems
I've written became
signposts. E.g. the last
poem of Scaffold of Jay;

the cup is the measure
of the vowel etc.

→
Swift made the identification
of the dogma of the
resurrection of the ~~dead~~ body
& spatialist theory.

→ The MA think of
time spatially. Eternity,
the nine stars, is spatialized
into a paradise, an
ordered space

Canadians, would be published by *white pelican,* where Sheila Watson was one of the journal's editorial collective (as he would later be) as well as its major financial backer. Only at the end of the 1970s, with the establishment of NeWest Press, with an editorial collective at that time largely from the University of Alberta and a mandate to publish western Canadian literature, and of Longspoon, a poetry press whose three editors were all also from the U of A, did he begin to publish a significant body of his work.

But how did he get from the invocation of *Friday's Child* —"Appear, O mother, was the perpetual cry / Of lost Aeneas" (*Poems* 9) — to Jenny Blake's letter to the Bachelor of Wire: "Of course some of this verse is fake. / And some of my love too. / Even sir for you" (*Poems* 107)? And how did he get from the Jenny Blake poems to this in *The Sorrowful Canadians*?

> **THE INVASION OF CANADA IS OVER**
> POEMS BEHIND THE SCENES ARE, WATER
> the invasion of Canada is over
> THE RIVER WATER IS ROTTEN (*Poems* 189)

A considered response might begin by looking to the long gestation of his first five-act play, *Cockcrow and the Gulls*, and what it taught him. Our goal in scrutinizing the process of writing this play is double: to understand something of the depth and complexity of the archive in relation to particular works and to understand something of how Watson, over his long apprenticeship, became the writer he did.

Man moves willfully
against his will

Facing page, top:
Outline for "Blyssop" from fall 1947 (91-459)

Facing page, bottom:
Watson's description of an evening spent with Blisset/Blyssop at the home of the Endicotts (91-01). Norman Endicott supervised Watson's thesis; Betty Endicott and Sheila Watson, who both taught at Moulton College, were friends.

The Long Apprenticeship in Drama

Beginnings of Cockcrow and the Gulls

The germs of two ideas that eventually shaped *Cockcrow* appear in 1947 notebook entries. The first outlines a life of "Blyssop" (91-459), a fictionalized William Blissett (91-06 Aug 14 1954). A fellow student with Watson at both UBC and Toronto, Blissett, with his mother, during the 1948–49 academic year shared the house the Watsons rented. The second is an idea for "Dialogues of the Dead" in which "Groups of the dead discuss themselves as things, as their past, as something they own, but are detached from" (91-459), that is, discuss themselves as do the objects in the riddles of the *Exeter Book*.

By mid-1952, both ideas were on the move. Blyssop, now Blossop, had become a character in a novel he sometimes titled "My Father"(and sometimes "The Double Life of Jeremy Patrick"). Its narrator is "the sorry child of the age which begins with Descartes & Locke & Newton" (91-06 June 20 1952). In some drafts Patrick is a professor at Cluny (a.k.a. Victoria College), in others an asylum inmate (July 29 1952). The novel was to be a satire on scientific rationalism as Watson understood *Tristram Shandy* to be, a satire on Romanticism, and a satire "on man's inability to learn from books," a lesson he took from *Don Quixote* (Aug 3 1952).

* Blyssop genuflects to Maryop.

* Blyssop crucifies himself.

* Blyssop, the true emulator
of Blake, the self-worshipper.

"I flatly deny yr. Reason, for
these reasons"

<u>Blyssop</u> I Birth II parentage
III his childhood IV his ~~p~~ education
V his friendships VI Blyssop as a
teacher VII in love.

– to be told in 1st person, this
person to be a foil.

– in vanity

– to be told as a string of anecdotes.

Yellow cornsheaf Ann, dewsweet, warm
smelling
Of the sun's breath, tall to man's breast
high,
Wheat for his garnering, ripe, blonde-falling
Thru farmer's fingers, seeds for his
fields to lie
Winterfallow for the furrow and spring-
plowing –
Springgreen for tommorrow and full of
increase:
Straw for his children's rompage & his
bed's ease.

Frost grind you Ann stone against
stone to dust
In Time's grim kitchen Bake ~~smoke~~ your yellow
grey
Squeeze ~~Turn~~ your saps sweetness from ~~and ingrat~~,
ingritted ~~incrust~~ grist
To the ~~te~~ ~~With~~ bitter ~~your~~ marrow, press yr ~~[illegible]~~
sunsap dry.
Until the corpse shall starve upon the
bone
The worm yet freshens, chilly bred upon

June 15, 47 Sunday Evening

S & I spent the evening with the Endicott's. When we were barely seated, and warming to one another, Miss Endicott, very <u>jeune fille</u>, came to the door, and, despite signals from Mrs. Endicott, refused to come in, and meet us; she blurted out message about the telephone, and fled. Endicott twitted me about Richardson's latest critic. Bussett expatiated at great length and <u>ex cathedra</u> on the relative merits of standard violin concertos, and of clarinet concertos; he was heard out patiently by Mrs. Endicott. He combines the face of a cherub, with the weight and pronouncement of Almighty God. A Mr. Towse ~~expatiated~~ accused the large book publishers of destroying the incipient talents of young authors. I maintained that the imposition of rigid, fixed requirements is not necessarily an insuperable obstacle to a clever writer.

Sunday, May 15, 1950. Last week the final examinations at UBC were wound up, a lugubrious affair, but especially so for me. I had ~~the~~ sense of being exiled. I have started on my thesis anew. This year I have written a great deal of poetry. I became more reconciled to my degree of poetry, of poetical talent, and have no delusions as to its rank. I believe I have some variety of voice.

I thought, as I always do, of writing a novel.

I conceived a point of view novel about a Mother Cummings (of Duncan or Chemainus), of her recent widowhood, of her son's inheritance, of his marriage to ~~Doris~~ a Mary Brown; of his success in business and his reversion to drink; of the way in which the mother Cummings blames Mary as unsuitable; of Mary's still-born child; of Doris, Joyce's sister at University; of her friendship with Peter Strick & her seduction — which wd be symbolized by a long description of the flight down to rock beach, where the sun mounting are; of Peter's Lovelace tastes — his friends Pawny, the Italian widow Pongo, etc, who all influence Doris; of Pawny who wants to paint her in the nude and of Peter's protection; of the bust-down by Pawny; of Doris's second child & of her reconciliation to Joyce; of Mother Cummings's reconciliation. Mother Cummings to be a good human.

22

The carenters (my father's disciple)
Jason, the servant and gravedigger
his wife, Medea.

Vancouver Island the asylum of the British Empire, convicts to Australia lunatics to Vanc. Is. Many lunatics in England, the climate, always changing, breeds them. Our climate perfects what England sends us.

My father's poetry. His professorship at Cluny, the college affiliated to University. Taught English, which was to him, first of all, theology, then philosophy, then science then anything whatsoever.

My father's grammar.

23

July 30 — The Double Life (of Jeremy Patrick).

I poet & criticisms & testimonials from the great
II Father & Son
III professor of EL at Cluny
— man the book-ridden
— Words with his prototype with his Book on the Follies of Books
— review of all the books & their false notions of man
— value of philosophy, that it shows us false avenues of thought
(cont.)
IV Vision of entrances
V The Saint — madness — death.

July 31, Aug 1 This morning I was awakened by a sudden down pouring of rain. The lighting flashing, and the wind striking the north of the house.

\# A tendency to explain moral evil in the universe in terms of immaturity of man

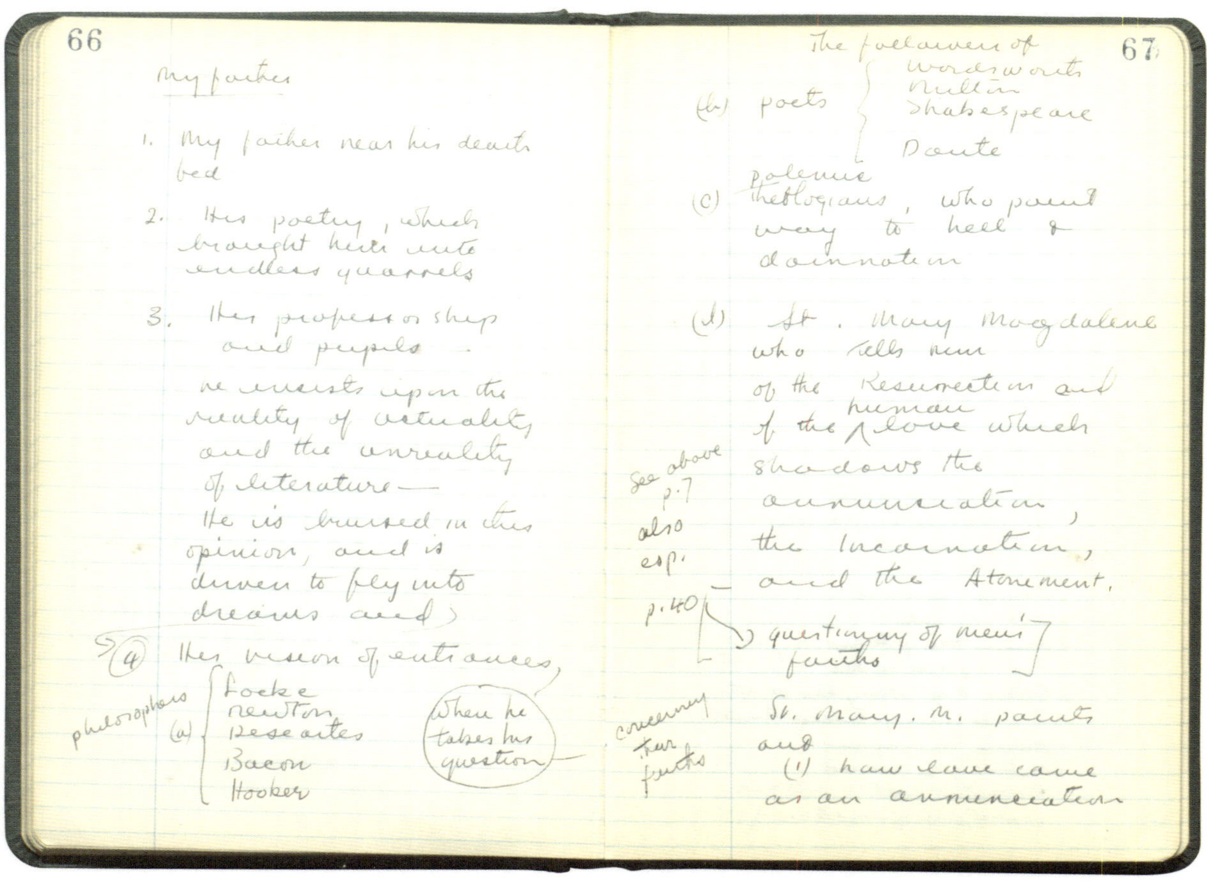

66

My father

1. My father near his death bed
2. His poetry, which brought him into endless quarrels
3. His professorship and pupils.
he insists upon the reality of actuality and the unreality of literature —
He is bruised in this opinion, and is driven to fly into dreams and)
(4) His vision of entrances, (When he takes his question)

philosophers (a) Locke, Newton, Descartes, Bacon, Hooker

67

The followers of
(b) poets: Wordsworth, Milton, Shakespeare, Dante
(c) polemic theologians, who point way to hell & damnation
(d) St. Mary Magdalene who tells him of the Resurrection and of the human love which shadows the annunciation, the Incarnation, and the Atonement.

See above p. 7 also esp. p. 40 — [questioning of men's faiths]

questioning their faiths — St. Mary M. paints and (1) how love came as an annunciation

Facing page, top:
"Convicts to Australia, lunatics to Vanc. Is.": "The Double Life of Jeremy Patrick," July 1952 (91-06)

Facing page, bottom:
Scenario for "My Father," early 1953 (91-06)

Below:
"Vision of Entrances," Aug 1952 (91-06)

"Dialogues of the Dead" had become "Vision of Entrances" "when the dead are seen making their entrances into that mode of eternity which they selected when in time"(Aug 11 1952). The theme is identical with one Marcel cites: "'In death we shall lay ourselves open to what we have lived on when we were on earth'" (II.186). Or as Boswell, Blyssop/Blossop's final avatar, puts it in *Cockcrow and the Gulls,* "Death, sir, is what you make it. . . . THERE they die the sort of death they lived in life" (*Plays* 64). That the topography of eternity resembles Dante's, with its wharf of the dead, mountain, desert, and chasm, owes something to Dorothy Sayers's verse translation of the *Inferno,* which Watson had discovered in February 1952 (95-190 WW to SW Jan 9 1952), and it also owes something to Charles Williams's *Paradiso* (91-06 Aug 11 1952).

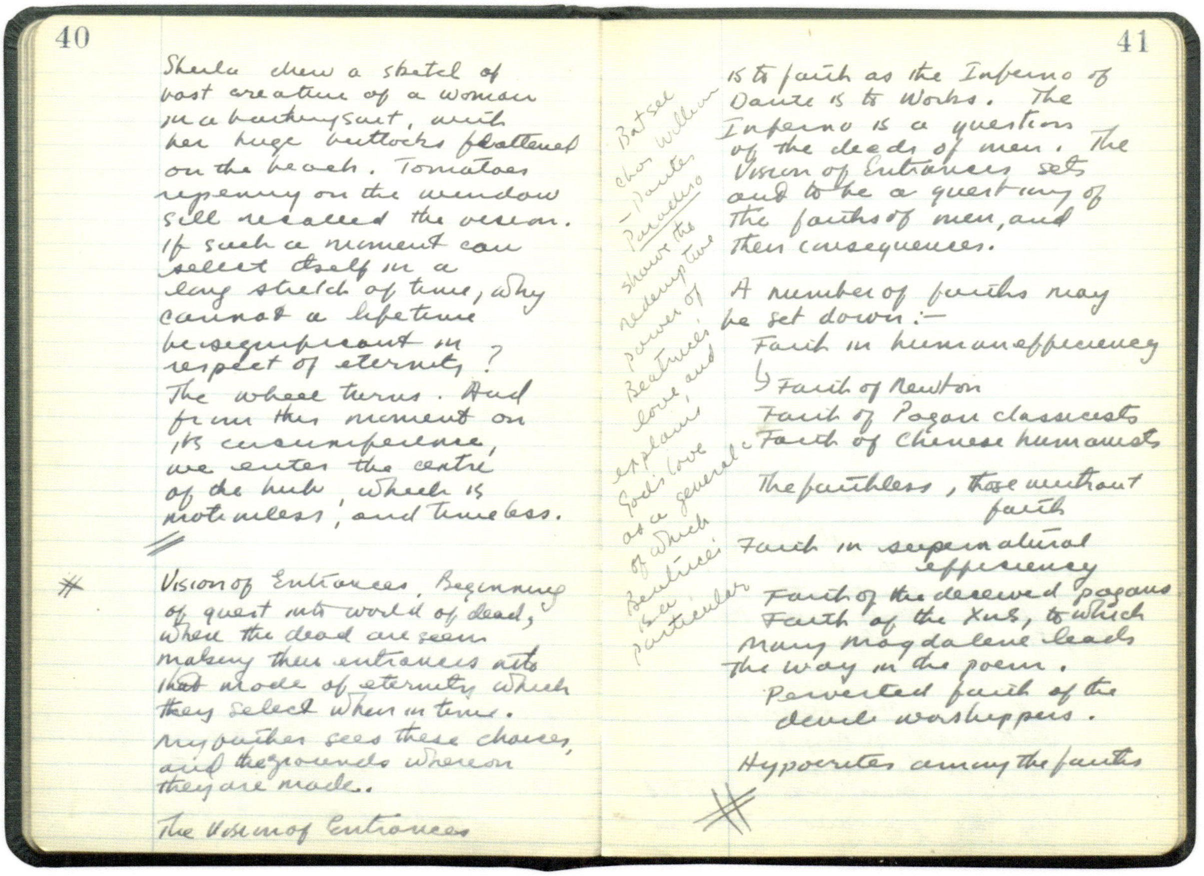

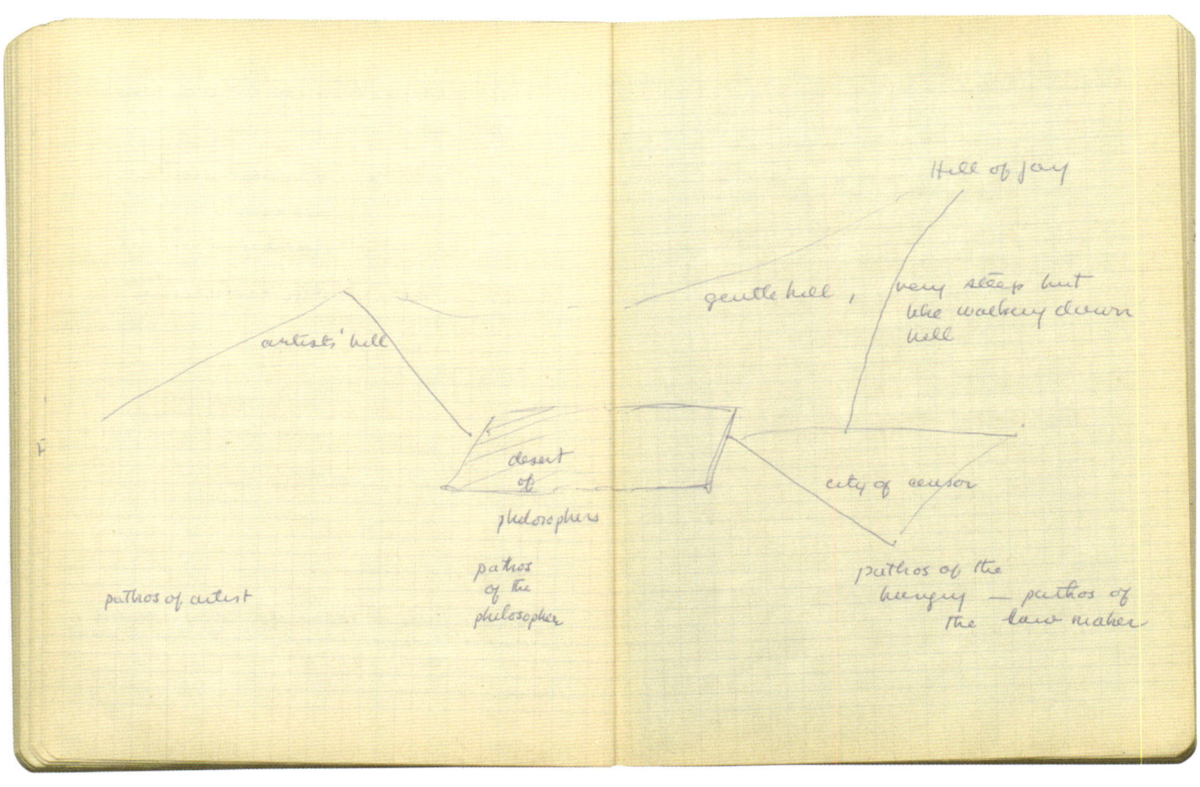

The topography of eternity, 1955–56
(91-50)

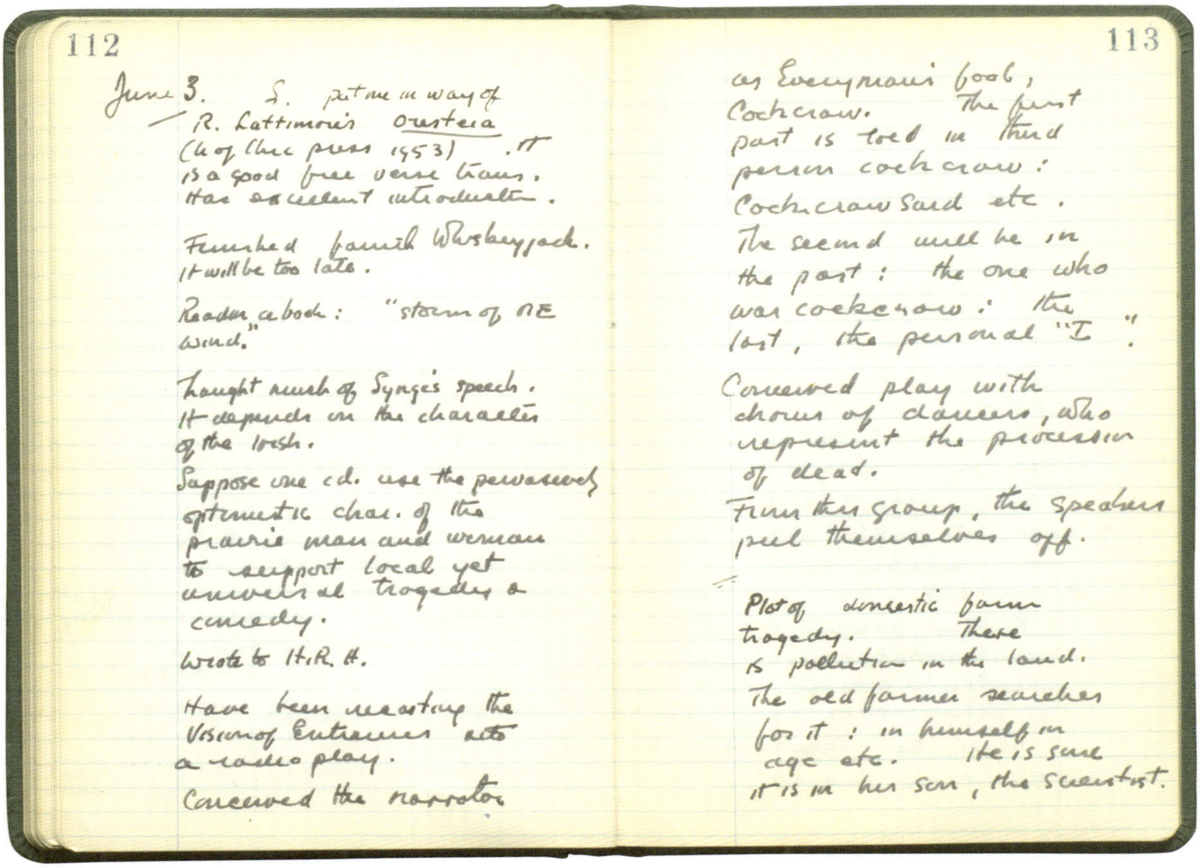

112

June 3. S. put me in way of
R. Lattimore's Oresteia
(U of Chic press 1953). It
is a good free verse trans.
Has excellent introduction.

Finished Journal Whiskeyjack.
It will be too late.

Reader, a book: "storm of NE
wind."

Thought much of Synge's speech.
It depends on the character
of the Irish.

Suppose one cd. use the pervasively
optimistic char. of the
prairie man and woman
to support local yet
universal tragedy & comedy.

Wrote to H.R.H.

Have been recasting the
Vision of Entrances into
a radio play.

Conceived the narrator

113

as Everyman's fool,
Cockcrow. The first
part is told in third
person cockcrow:
Cockcrow said etc.
The second will be in
the past: the one who
was cockcrow: the
last, the personal "I".

Conceived play with
chorus of dancers, who
represent the procession
of dead.

From this group, the speakers
peel themselves off.

Plot of domestic farm
tragedy. There
is pollution in the land.
The old farmer searches
for it: in himself in
age etc. He is sure
it is in his son, the scientist.

"Everyman's fool, Cockcrow" arrives on the scene (91-06)

In June 1952 Watson thought of combining these two works and the following January drafted a scenario that sees Patrick on his deathbed having a "vision of entrances" that includes seventeenth- and eighteenth-century scientists and philosophers and concludes with Mary Magdalene telling "him of the Resurrection and of the human love which shadows the [A]nnunication, the Incarnation and the Atonement" (91-06 Jan 1953). By Good Friday that year, she brings with her "the magic pearl." Along the way, he has drafted a scenario for "Story of Two Coats," based on Xenophon, with a Cockney character, 'Enri 'Ighgate (91-06 Aug 1 1952).

By the summer of 1953, then, Watson, still a long way from *Cockcrow and the Gulls,* was working with some of its basic ideas — the vision of life after death, the meaning of the Resurrection, the pearl of great price[19]/pearl of communion that one could receive only by giving it up — and with the character of the demotic Cockney, the common man who would be king (Lear). He returned to "Vision of Entrances" in the summer of 1954, rich with ideas. He recorded "recasting" it as a radio play (91-06 June 3 1954), as prose (Oct 8 1954), and as a Passion play (Aug 14 1954). In a decisive moment the character Cockcrow arrived on the scene: "Conceived the narrator as Everyman's fool, Cockcrow. . . . Conceived play with chorus of dancers, who represent the procession of the dead" (June 3 1954). Six months later he read Tyrell on psychical research[20] and, "unsatisfied" with that writer's "glimpse of the nature of death," reversed him: "I saw death in terms of life" (Oct 23 to Nov 13 1954). Enter another central idea of *Cockcrow*: that "The final moment of birth is death. Thus the life pangs and death pangs are birth pangs" (Jan 27 1955). He had already found the idea in Marcel, who had concluded that when a person's self-sacrifice or dedication to a cause beyond himself led to death, that "death might be really, and in a supreme sense, life" (I.167). As Watson would put it some three years later: "The crucifixion asserts the love of God, for the death of Christ is the nativity, the birth is in the crucifixion" (91-21 Mar 28 1958).

In the summer of 1954, the question of poetic speech occupied him: "as Marcel reminds us," he wrote, "the anti-poetic is the true subject matter of the poet. . . . On the other hand, the central life of our day — the city life — is, if full of the most anti-poetic stuff, also full of its own poetry — the speech, etc. . . . It is this central subject matter which I want to deal with" (91-06 May 26 1954; Marcel I.45). Much of his struggle during the long gestation of *Cockcrow* would be the attempt "to try to speak in verse, not to find a sort of verse which seems like prose speech" — that is, to get past Shakespeare's blank verse and Eliot's verse drama (91-25 Sept 1 1958).

The wheel dance (91-08)

By late 1954 Watson had "conceived of a dramatic way of dealing with 'Vision of Entrances'" material. "Cockcrow tells his story (as one from the dead) to his five cronies, who have sent him out to drink himself drunk" (91-6 Nov 13 1954). By January, he

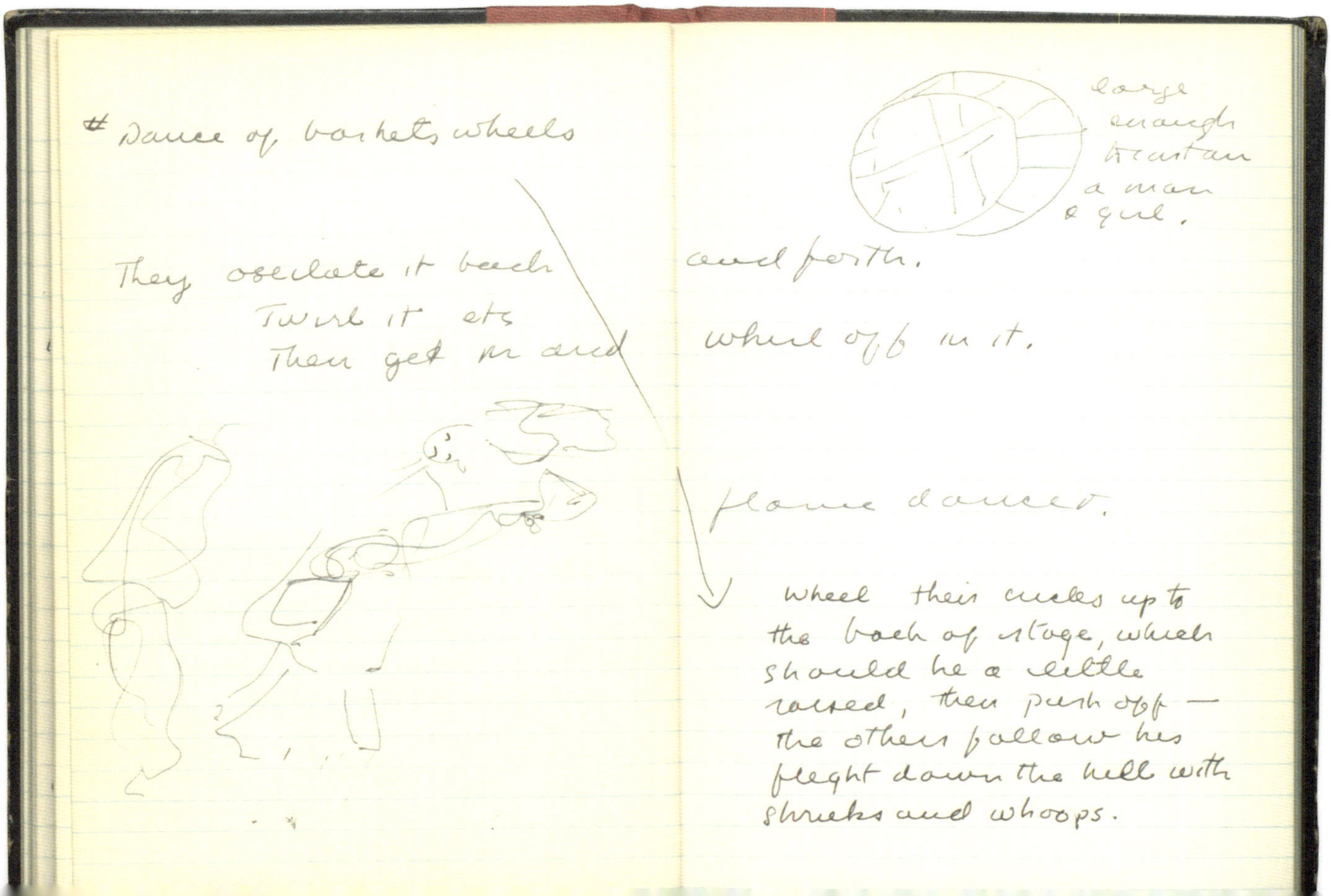

April 8, 1955. I cannot write what day it is.
I set down these proverbs:—
The farmer sifts wheat from the husk.
The man who plants a tree saves the stone, but he doesn't spit out the fruit.
The farmer doesn't want land. He wants the fruits of the land.

—//—

I have been meditating the new conception of the city. It is a city of justice and vice.— With the possibility of the perversion of will of the city goes the city code. This code is not so much regulatory, as one of the vices of the city. If pride is a royal sin, greed a commercial sin — then

19

Pharisaism is the civic sin. The whole episode starts with a dance.
I am in a quandary about how to represent the matter dramatically. (1) Could it all be done as imagined outscene? (2) Could the city be represented in pantomime? (3) Could the city be enacted in scene? On the whole, I think it will have to be done more or less in scene. That is the more dramatic way, where action and poetry balance. The inscene technique is more 'poetical'. I think of the York crucifixion.
S. asked me about the dates of Shakespeare. I didn't know them. I

Good Friday, 1955;
The City of the Dead
(91-09)

had drafted an outline for a "new Cockcrow." That draft gave him grief over the next years as he tried to deal with an allegorical Masque of the City derived from "Vision of Entrances" and from his reading of Marcel. The Masque satirized world politics, urban planning, scientific "mechanism," and humankind's "perversion of the will." At various times it included miners of the river of ice, a dialogue of builders and architects, a fire dance, a scene of lovers, dancers spinning themselves in the wheels of their will, a Mayor's banquet for union workers, a Carnival of Animals, and Boswell's introductions to the famous and infamous. These last included scientists, philosophers, and poets, but also Hitler, Mussolini, Stalin, Franco, and three little girls from Hiroshima. The play had too many agendas, too many themes, too many targets. Allegory strangled drama. Still, Watson reflected a few months later, "The city is forcing me to consider the problem of stage properties as symbols" (91-10 Dec 12 1955).

Despite the difficulties attendant on this draft, Watson slowly clarified two ideas that govern the play: that men "recrucify daily" "the love of God for man" (91-06 Jan 9 1955) and that "the will and its perversion" drives to despair (Jan 27 1955). "The essence of the crucifixion," he wrote, "is the Giving himself of God to man. And in a sense every gift of God to man is a type of the crucifixion. Hence, so is every gift of man to woman, or man to man" (91-9 Apr 30 1955). Furthermore, "the myth knows that this crucifixion is an always. The crucifixion is now. It is part of the eternal relation of man and God" (June 2 1955). The Crucifixion became the single most important symbol of his work: it runs, for example, through the poetry of *The Sorrowful Canadians* and determines the structure and action of his last completed play, *Gramsci x 3*.

Facing page:
"The new Cockcrow,"
Jan 1954 (91-06)

The second idea about the perversion of the will, derived from Marcel, he struggled to articulate:

> All I can hope for, as my meaning, is an irony. . . . I see the irony between exultation in furious, willful activity and the Christian end of man. . . . Perhaps I might further state my own proposed irony: that which is perceived when a man tortures himself to act and turns himself into a hurtling stone, when he could move easily as an angel flies. Man moves willfully against his will. . . . (91-06 Mar 12 1955)

In his drafts an enacted metaphor initially served: the dead curl their wills inside wheels, hurtle down a slope, push their wheels back up, and hurtle down again . . . and again . . . and again . . .

In February 1955 Watson introduced an ironic insight he subsequently lost, then rediscovered: "I saw clearly my Cockcrow story as the comedy of revelation. The ghost with all to tell, but the beholders are unwilling to hear. Then, the actual revelation made with Cockcrow as the unwitting instrument" (Feb 21 1955). In February, too, he reminded himself that "Cockcrow" was to be a "Mystery play cycle." He drafted an extended scenario with a prologue spoken by the Seven Vices, and a plot in which the "inmates" of the brothel, led by the Cockney Higgins, debate the nature of death; Higgins's son Cyril, "in the name of piety, upbraids" them; Cockcrow vows to get dead drunk so as to "speak from knowledge of death"; the defrocked priest O'Reilly relates Cockcrow's death; Cockcrow returns; Boswell takes the inmates to the City of the Dead; there is a trial; the "youth who calls himself Christ is crucified;" O'Reilly commits suicide; and the prostitute Greta brings the pearl and tells of her dream of the Nativity (91-08 Feb 26 1955).

Although Watson will add elements such as the murder of Mrs. Higgins to this plot over the next years, will make telling modifications such as having his characters crucify a scarecrow rather than a youth, and will delete nearly all the stops on Boswell's tour of the City of the Dead, at this juncture he has arrived at a plot to which he will stick. In early May, he noted that "I have with some agony managed to start a few pages of Cockcrow" (91-07 May 3 1955). It would take him more than six years to complete.

... the year in Paris ...

IN AUGUST 1955 Wilfred Watson arrived in Paris, courtesy of a Department of Foreign Affairs Overseas Fellowship.[21] His application had been to work on his play and to study French drama, particularly medieval drama, which, he thought, "could be as fruitful for modern drama as the study of the ballad was fruitful for Romantic poetry" (95-395 WW to J.T. Jones Mar 25 1959). His interest lay neither in French classical theatre nor in the declamatory tradition of the Comédie Française; he seems to have attended only two of its productions: Racine's *Britannicus*, to which Gabriel Marcel took him (91-234 Oct 23 1978), and Molière's *Le Misanthrope* (SW-9 July 22 1956). While he had a letter of introduction to Monsieur Perrault, the theatre's director, he does not record using it (91-12 Sept 10 1955); indeed the only meeting in Paris that either he or Sheila Watson notes his having sought was with Gabriel Marcel (SW-3 Sept 20 1955).

Part of what interested him in both medieval and contemporary French drama was its eschewal of elaborate sets and staging and of declamation and stylized gesture. Jacques Copeau had launched contemporary French theatre in 1913 by opening the Théâtre du Vieux-Colombier and there insisting on simple sets and staging and on natural speech and movement. His disciple, Charles Dullin, in 1921 established his own troupe at L'Atelier in Montmartre and his own school, the École Nouvelle du Comédien, where he trained actors in movement, improvisation and mime. Watson, who read Lucien Arnaud's book about

Wilfred Watson, Paris; photograph taken at request of Faber and Faber by Studio Berthès, Paris (95-24-04)

Facing page:
Opposite a citation from Simone Weil on the evil perpetrated by the justice system, Watson made this attempt to reproduce Renoir's *Gabrielle à blouse ouverte*, Oct 29 1955 (91-12).

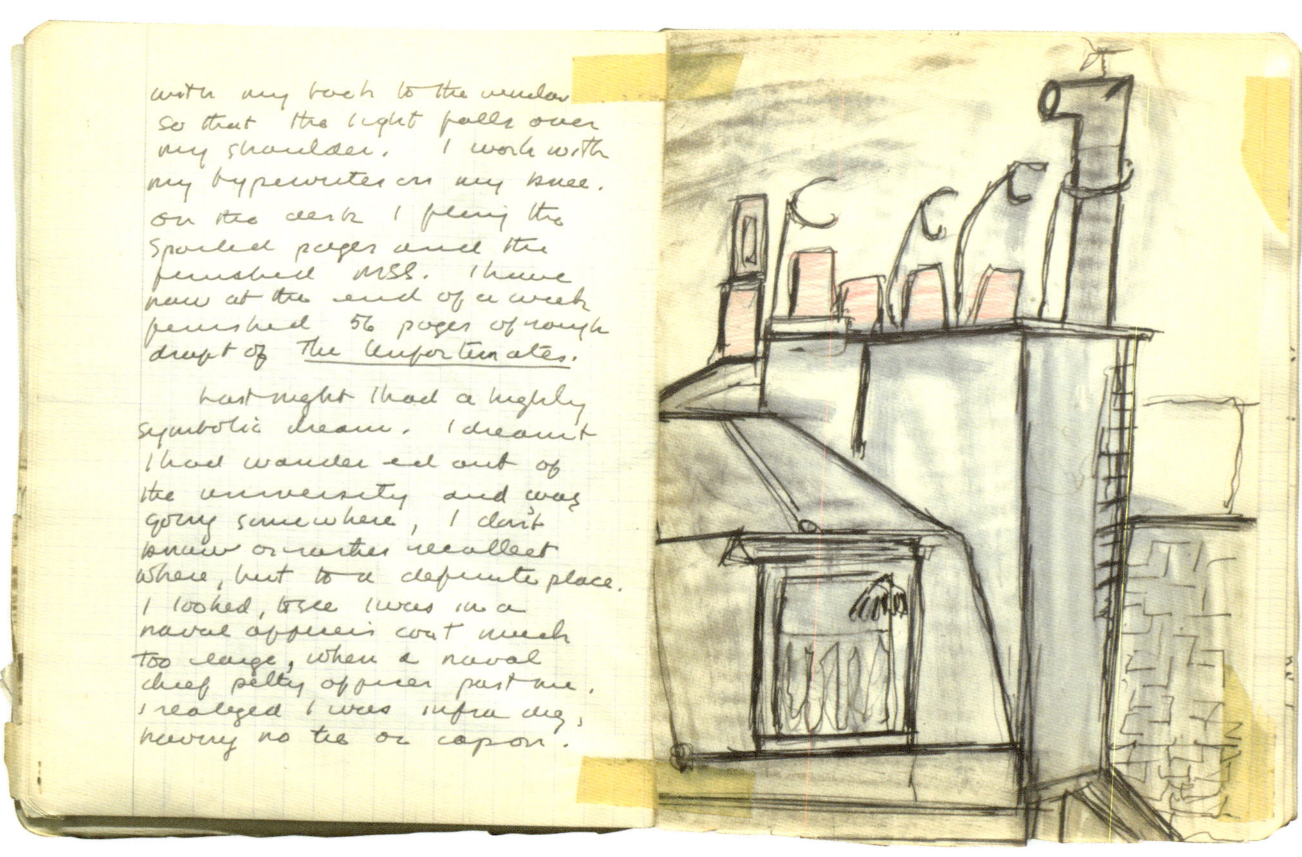

with my back to the window so that the light falls over my shoulder. I work with my typewriter on my knee. On the desk I fling the spoiled pages and the finished MSS. I have now at the end of a week finished 56 pages of rough draft of The Unfortunates.

Last night I had a highly symbolic dream. I dreamt I had wandered out of the university and was going somewhere, I don't know or rather recollect where, but to a definite place. I looked, to see I was in a naval officer's coat much too large, when a naval chief petty officer past me, I realized I was infra dig, having no tie or cap on.

Watson's drawing of the view from his Paris apartment (91-12)

Dullin's work (91-17 July 18 1955), took to heart the aims of Dullin's instruction: in the words of a later commentator, the École Nouvelle du Comédien aimed "to establish a register of the dramatic resources of the human body. . . . the actor taken as a psycho-physiological whole, is the dough of the play, the matter out of which it is made" (Lorelle 55). Watson would adopt wholeheartedly this precept about the role of the actor as co-creator of the play. In a "Draft Preface for Cockcrow," a manifesto prepared while the play was in rehearsal, he would assert: "dramatic verse has for its chief role . . . the detonation of the actor into gesture, movement, and dance" (91-72).

He began his Paris theatre-going with the *Oresteia* cycle presented in André Obey's French adaptation at the Théâtre Marigny by Madeleine Renaud and Jean-Louis Barrault's company; Barrault was Dullin's most famous student. Watson not only purchased the very expensive collection of critical essays published on the occasion of the production,[22] but attended each of the three plays twice. Much later, he credited the production with starting him "thinking about the chorus" as "multiple voices" (91-286 draft letter to unidentified recipient). He would see Barrault perform twice more: in Vauthier's monologue, *Le Personnage combattant,* and in Jules Supervielle's *Les suites d'une course*, an absurdist play that sees a man transformed into a horse and back again.

166

we are misfits in the world and until we see this, we suffer. Suffering may not be said to open our eyes. But it puts us in an asking condition.

March 11
A beautiful sunny day. Thought of a dramatic farce, The Girl who read Marcel Aymé.

Act I
In which Lisa changes her husband into an elephant.

Act II In which she admits she has changed him into an elephant.

Act III In which she asks the director of the zoo to allow

167

her to change her husband back into a man.
Refusal
She changes the director into an elephant.

Act IV She changes them both back.

Act I Lisa comes back with her newlywed husband John from Marcel Aymé's Oiseaux de Lune. Her matter of fact husband points out to her how impossible it all is: sheer nonsense. She insists it is very possible. He asks how. She explains, (1) by hypnosis (2) by the power of the imagination. He

Scenario for "The Girl who read Marcel Aymé" (91-10)

The Watsons attended or heard broadcasts of various, mostly contemporary, plays during their eleven months in Paris. Pursuing his interest in contemporary uses of the morality play, they went to a Passion play acted by the workmen in the parish of Saint-Pierre de Ménilmont and to Robert Rey's *Le Mystère de Saint Caraman*. Both disappointed. Sacha Piteoff's adaptation of Gorky's *The Lower Depths* proved more satisfying, as did Sartre's *Huis Clos*, George Neveux's adaptation of Lope de Vega in *Le Chien du jardinier*, and Joan Littlewood's Theatre Workshop touring production of *The Good Soldier Schweik*. He attended at least one performance by the mime Marcel Marceau. He heard radio broadcasts of Sartre's *Les Mouches* and of Henri de Montherlant's *Port Royal*.[23]

He read at least two of the novelists associated with the absurd, Camus and Beckett, and attended several performances of theatre of the absurd works: the Supervielle play already noted, Jean Anouilh's *L'Ornifle*, Jacques Audiberti's *Le Mal Court*, Ionesco's *Les Chaises* and *L'Impromptu d'Alma*, Beckett's *Waiting for Godot*, and Marcel Aymé's *Les Oiseaux de la lune*. After seeing the Aymé play he drafted his own riff on the

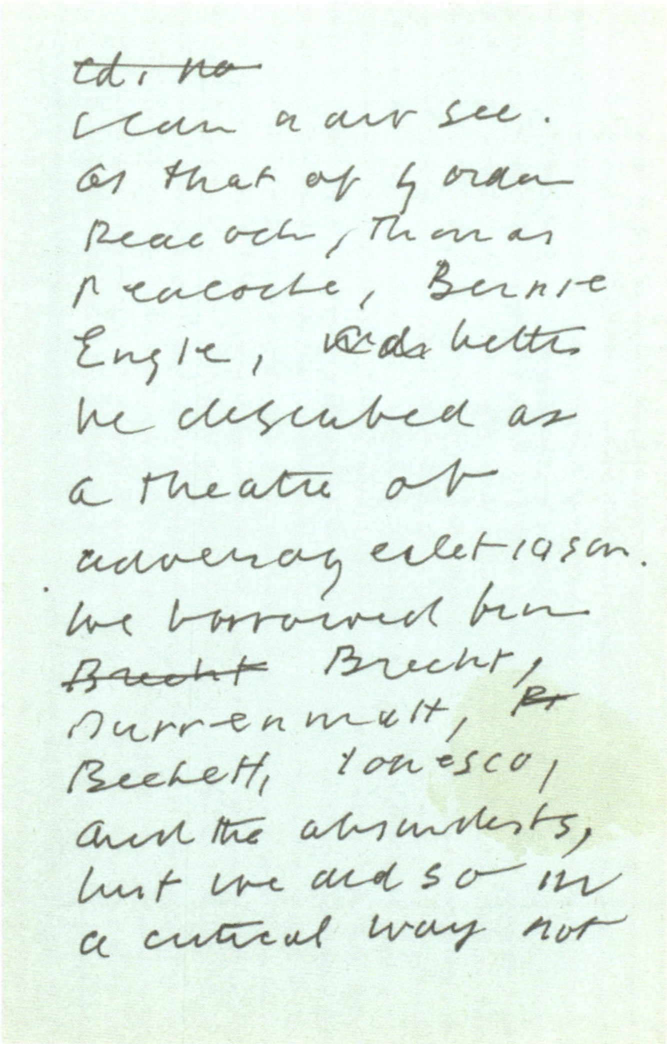
As that of Gordon
Peacock, Thomas
Peacocke, Bernie
Engle,
he described as
a theatre of
We borrowed from
Brecht,
Durrenmatt,
Beckett, Ionesco,
and the absurdists,
but we did so in
a critical way not

Watson, on Studio Theatre and theatre of the absurd, written while preparing *Plays at the Iron Bridge* (95-130)

theme of transformation, "The Girl who read Marcel Aymé," which, on his return, he "read" with Maurice Rabotin, a lecturer in the Department of Modern Languages and Literature, with whom he planned to collaborate in the writing of French dialogue (95-190a, WW to SW Nov 15 1956). He would work on the play sporadically until he gave "Is there an elephant in the house?" to Gordon Peacock (91-334 July 6 1962). Its action is precipitated when, returning from a performance of *Les Oiseaux de la lune,* a man insists on the absurdity of a plot that sees people changed into birds, only to learn how wrong he is when his wife hypnotizes him into an elephant. The first transformation entails others; elephants proliferate. As in Aymé, human order is eventually restored. A year after he gave this script to Gordon Peacock and after the production of *Cockcrow and the Gulls,* by which time theatre of the absurd was widely performed in North America, Watson would describe himself as "trying . . . to keep clear of the new orthodoxies, especially orthodoxies of the absurd" (91-73 Mar 29 1963). This did not signal a disdain of the absurd but rather a sharp disagreement with Esslin's argument that theatre of the absurd was about the exhaustion of language. For Watson the word — language — was primary and needed always to be meaningful.

What Watson initially did during his stay in Paris was write fiction. He worked through the autumn on a much earlier idea (91-06 July 18 1952) for a series of linked short stories, "The Misfits," themed on Hamlet's observation that "bad begins, worse remains behind." He completed a satirical novel, "The Rabbit's Paw." His "Cockcrow" workbooks during these months show him attempting to clarify the action of the play. He outlined the "Shakespearean conversions" — Higgins as Lear and common man,

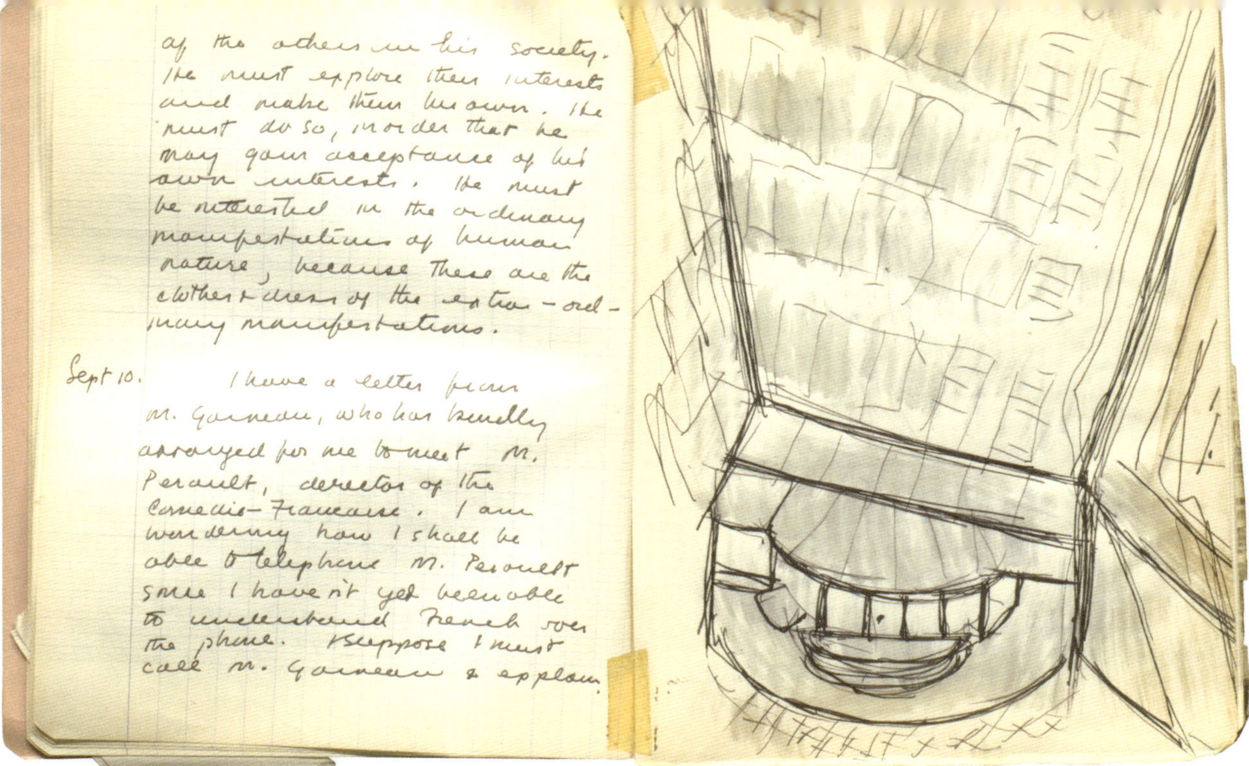

of the others in his society. He must explore their interests and make them his own. He must do so, in order that he may gain acceptance of his own interests. He must be interested in the ordinary manifestations of human nature, because these are the clothes & dress of the extra-ordinary manifestations.

Sept 10. I have a letter from M. Garneau, who has kindly arranged for me to meet M. Perault, director of the Comedie-Francaise. I am wondering how I shall be able to telephone M. Perault since I haven't yet been able to understand French over the phone. I suppose I must call M. Garneau & explain

Watson's drawing of the view of the inner courtyard from the couple's apartment, with an Art Deco roof over the shop that Sheila Watson would later discover had once been Henri Kahnweiler's famous gallery (91-12)

Cockcrow as Hamlet and Everyman's Fool, the newest prostitute, Iris, as Cordelia (91-08). He decided Higgins would murder his wife and Cyril be blinded, elements of plot he would retain, as well as that the masques would be "dreams" and that the prostitutes would be sentenced, à la Hester Prynne, to march around the City of the Dead three times wearing the letter *P*, ideas he would later drop.

Only during the last three months of his Paris stay did he work systematically on *Cockcrow*. He concentrated initially on the trial scene, with its theme, which he derived from an analysis of *Measure for Measure*, that "men, in order to punish, create even worse crimes than the ones they punish" (91-17 July 7 1956). That theme, with the trial as its emblem, became one of the most important recurrent motifs in his work. He began to focus more on the play's overall structure and outlined for himself the "patterns" defining the characters and the turning points in the play.

Prior to his time in Paris, Watson had seen almost no professional theatre. Canadian theatre of the 1940s and '50s was staged mostly by enthusiastic, occasionally gifted amateurs, Watson among them, sometimes led by a semi-professional or professional actor/director such as Gordon Peacock and Thomas Peacocke. In Paris he had his most intense experience of contemporary plays staged by professional companies with superb professional actors who were helping to transform contemporary theatre. He took lessons about dramatic conflict and pacing, structure and staging, chorus and characterization. Those lessons enabled him successfully to complete *Cockcrow and the Gulls*. But not right away.

... what he learned there ...

ON HIS RETURN TO CANADA IN AUGUST 1956, Watson let *Cockcrow* lie fallow, returning to it with intensity only in early 1958. His notebooks for the intervening eighteen months are filled with reflections on what he wanted to achieve, reflections on which his Paris writing, reading, and theatre-going had a good deal of bearing. What had he learned about playwriting? Four preoccupations recur: point-of-view narration versus what he later called "non-narrative dramatic immediacy" (91-40 Oct 15 1960); the use of colloquial speech in verse drama; the relation of speech to gesture; and "transfigurative mimesis" (91-20 Aug 30 1957).

On finishing "the first very rough draft" of his aborted novel, "The Misfits," he had returned to a quarrel with James's "point of view" novel:

> I wish to tell a story as a man tells an account of a battle he was engaged in. I do not want to do as Henry James does, create an illusion that the reader is present <u>at</u> the battle and engaged in the struggle going on. . . . James . . . does for the reader what the reader can do himself.
> (91-12 Oct 2 1955)

When he had first enunciated this disagreement in May 1952, he had concluded: "I'd like a novel to be a simple statement, on the surface. But to imply the drama beyond. Some popular writers can do this" (91-07). Still worrying the question of the reader, in November he puzzled over Wyndham Lewis's *Monstre Gai*, asking himself, "Might [Lewis's] point have been more forceful if made less obliquely — if made for the common reader, not the professional detective? Hasn't this been a great fault of our age, the writing which requires almost a superhuman intelligence to understand?" (91-50 Nov 19 1955). Implicit in this questioning of James and Lewis is Watson's own populism and his movement towards the presentation of his material as immediate rather than mediated by either "point of view" or the writer's cleverness.

"Non-narrative dramatic immediacy" entailed recommitment to the use of an "anti-poetic" material and required "a style that is easy and flexible and fairly casual — perhaps above all free of the characteristic clichés of English and American Mandarinism. But avoiding the danger of Hemingway beer-bottle phrases" (91-12

Oct 23 1955). He would not, as he heard Eliot doing, speak "as if we find an inspiration in conversation & colloquial speech for poetry," but would "learn how to speak colloquially in the verse forms" he used (91-20 Oct 10 1957). His colloquial style would treat "an essentially tense subject matter" (91-12 Oct 9 1955). Plays such as *Les Chaises* — in which the husband calls his wife *mon chou* while speaking to their fantasized guests with exaggerated formality — or *Waiting for Godot* — which Watson understood as using conversation as "an art of killing time" (91-17 July 21 1957) — must have reinforced his conviction, already apparent in 1954 when he had set the Irish "blather" of O'Reilly against the Cockney "blather" of Higgins (91-37 Aug 9 1960), that contrast in characters' language could provide important dramatic tension. It could also introduce playfulness and absurdity; one character's discourse could seem to another "like the Agnus Dei set to the tune of Yes, we have no bananas" (91-08 Feb 1955). But above all, verse drama was the poetry of the "thinking heart": "Dramatic poetry — drama — goes beyond dance and music to transcend, not destroy emotion, but to clarify it with ideas" (91-17 Sept 1956).

Word and gesture
(95-04)

* In theatre of the absurd, we have the art of the translated word and the dubbed in gesture. The gesture is matched to the wrong word. In Waiting for Godot, the gesture is that of a clown, the words the words of existentialism. The lack of correlation is the absurd.

* theatre of the absurd comes right out of translated theatre, with its ersatz words and dubbed in gesture. It turns a vice into a virtue.

* ~~we cannot have~~ I would like to put word and gesture into meaningful relationship.

Near the end of his Paris stay, Watson began to think intently about the relationship of gesture to speech. He had seen a good deal of mime. He attended performances by a Kabuki troupe and by Marcel Marceau. Barrault acted the man but mimed the horse in *Les suites d'une course*. Watson took particular note of Jean Martin's mimed performance of the hotel waiter in *Le Personnage combattant*. All of this led to his "invention of . . . mime cues. . . . These are an extension of stage directions, which are as ineffective as directions on a package of patent food." Mime cues supplied "a secondary channel by which a play's meaning can be developed. The contrast between this and the channel of speeches could create an extremely useful tension" (91-17 May 12 1956). He drafted sections of the play with mime cues: "You are feeling the strength of your arms, of your legs. Your arms, your legs. You are angry, Cyril. . . . You are trying to wrench your body away from your father, Higgins. . . . You have a pistol, Cyril. Take it out. You are trying to persuade yourself you can use it on Higgins" (91-51). He proceeded immediately to a draft without mime cues, but the idea had done its work; he began to think more carefully about the relation of gesture and word, and about how to minimize stage directions in favour of dialogue that in itself gave rise to actors' gestures. When he completed the next draft of the play, he would remind himself that "stage business becomes crucial. . . . In a good play, the lines shd never need stage business applied as an *appliqué*. I.e. the mime of the actor shd follow naturally from the speeches or rise naturally against them" (Dec 23 1958). He measured his success thus far against Shakespeare.

Almost a year after he returned to the writing of *Cockcrow* in January 1958, this recognition led to one of his fullest definitions of *poetic drama*. "Poetic drama = mime x verse," he explained to himself:

> Mime makes visual & spatial whereas verse makes auditory — the things of the heart & mind, i.e. experience.
>
> . . . The essence of poetic drama, then, is a counterpointing of mime and verse so that at one apprehension we see what we hear, and we hear what we see. (91-27 Nov 21 1958)

By the time he completed *Cockcrow* he had arrived at a definition of drama as "the conflict between the rhetoric of words and the revelation of gesture or/and the conflict between formal gesture and the mimicry of life in words. The fabric of drama is embarrassment of words by gesture" (91-58 Jan 1961).

The French plays Watson saw not only reinforced and extended his thinking about narration, colloquial speech, and gesture; they moved him toward what he called "transfigurative mimesis." He worried less about his characters' motivations and over the next years removed motivations such as the murders he had once had the prostitutes commit, on the grounds that as soon as the playwright had "to give the backgrounds of the characters in order that they be characters, the drama is clogged" (91-17 Feb 10 1957). Perhaps most importantly, theatre of the absurd showed Watson some ways in which he could dramatically realize Marcel's concept of intersubjectivity. The theatre of Ionesco and Beckett does not demand that its audience empathize with their characters; rather, it requires that that the audience be fully present in the action of the play. When in *Les Chaises* the elderly concierge and his wife welcome imaginary guests who are invisible to the audience, that audience must itself receive those guests into its consciousness and supply their half of the conversation. While Vladimir and Estragon wait, the audience waits. The participation, even the complicity, of the audience need not be secured by flattery; the play could, as Watson sometimes understood *Cockcrow* to do, "flaunt" and "insult" rather than "flatter" the audience into intersubjectivity (91-24 June 16 1958).

Watson, however, took the realization of intersubjectivity in drama well beyond theatre of the absurd to arrive at a "transfigurative mimesis." "Poetry," he asserted, is a "shape-giving element in life itself." He tested this hypothesis against Shakespeare, who "is dramatic in that he projects into the lap <u>of his audience</u> the transfiguration he attempts" (91-20 Aug 30 1957). Watson made his fullest statement of what he had come to understand as intersubjectivity in poetry and drama a little over a year after his return from Paris. It drew heavily on Gabriel Marcel:

> Art is not primarily contemplative. It is not a 'seeing' nor a 'looking for.' . . . We see only as we act, and if we act and suffer cognitively, as perhaps we do when we enter into a work of art, the end of the work of art is . . . a bodily consciousness, the body becoming mind and the mind becoming body. In Gabriel Marcel's phrase, art is intersubjective.
>
> The key art is drama. At a performance . . . we enter . . . into the life of the chief chars., we enter into the lives of the actors who represent these characters, we enter into the life of the author — into that of the audience who share experience with us — we theirs, they ours.
>
> So with a lyric poem. The reader is producer, director, actor, audience. . . . the poet . . . must provide his reader with a vehicle into which he has projected himself and into which the reader-actor can project himself too, as an actor puts himself into a part in a play.
>
> . . . A poetic experience merely becomes a true poem if by means of the formal structures the poet can project experience in such a way that the reader (the reader as actors) can participate in the life of the poet. (91-20 Oct 14 1957)

the imagination. (Hence the truth of Shakespeare's "We are such stuff as dreams are made on.") In other words, it is the imagination which feeds on sense, but the feast is always periodic. For the mind is temporal and sequential, whereas sensation is of that which is non-sequential. Even though that which is sensed may be transient, of the world of Plato's becoming.

McLuhan's idea that the silent reading age is the revolutionary age. It puts the reader in the circle of his imagination. It makes him individualist. The Russian who lives in the circle of sense: he agrees but is opposite.

There are indeed three circles.

circle of imagination

circle of sense

circle of discursive reason

Action occurs when the three circles are in connection. Hence, when

Aristotle calls drama an imitation of an action, he confuses. An action doesn't occur until it is dramatic, i.e., when all the three circles intersect. Hence, to call drama an imitation of action, is to call it an imitation of itself.. Very circular — is my punishment?

But isn't all this contra ordinary usage?
An imagination is one thing.
An action is another.
A judgement is another.

Hence, it shd be: circle of imagination, the circle of sensual action, the circle of discursive judgement.
When these intersect, one finds the intersect of dramatic action, the drama, or play: but the novel belongs to the circle of imagination.
Quaere: what, epistemologically,

Three circles (91-17)

Two years later, when he approached the final draft of *Cockcrow and the Gulls*, he focused yet again on art as transfiguration: in transfiguration, "there are four things related, the artist, the universe, the work of art, and the spectator. And the nature of a work of art is to effect changes, according to the imperium of the artist, in all four" (91-31 Sep 12 1959). Moving from theory to praxis, he diagrammed himself doing this through the intersection in drama of three overlapping circles: a "circle of sense," understood, as in Marcel, as feelings experienced as inseparable from our bodies; "a circle of imagination," understood as McLuhan's reader (of novels); and "a circle of discursive reason" (91-17 Apr–June 12 1957). Or, as he put it two years later, "What is necessary — now — is to get mind back into drama, and poetry" (91-29 Apr 27 1959).

... the long apprenticeship continued ...

ON RETURNING TO HIS PLAY IN JANUARY 1958, Watson affirmed its "playfulness" as necessary to its Christian allegory of the artist. He addressed a number of issues of structure, pacing, and production. And he thought through a number of dramatic techniques that he would use in most of the plays that came after *Cockcrow.*

Although we have seen that Watson valued what he understood to be the myth of Christianity, and particularly its central event, the Crucifixion, for its symbolic and allegorical potential, his notebooks make clear his intellectual and moral contempt for institutionalized religion. Sometimes they make plain his unbelief: "Of the two drugs, baseball and Xty, I suppose, in the scale of sedation, baseball to score more highly" (91-239 Oct 17 1979), he wryly observed as he was structuring *Gramsci x 3* around the Stations of the Cross. Yet, throughout his notebooks of the 1950s, with their many meditations on the meaning of Original Sin and of the Crucifixion, or on the nature of the Darkness preceding God's creation of Light, he often leaves the impression that he writes as a believer. Whether or not he believed in Christian doctrine, what is certain is that in his notebooks he reflects from *within* the allegory he has adopted. A return to his manifesto of "religion for art's sake" can perhaps situate us, if only temporarily, in relation to Watson's "God":

> One doesn't invent a religion. One finds out what one's religion is.
>
> Because we find truth only in works of art — by truth we mean what is eternally as it is. The Grecian urn, as long as it exists, is eternally the truth that is the Grecian urn. . . .
>
> Because there are many works of art, and all so different, we believe in an incomprehensible God. This God has the wisdom which passes all understanding — in fact, is to human reason utterly absurd. God is the absurd. We believe in him passionately. (91-20 Feb 13 1960)

Watson found his religion in the transfigurative mimesis of art. He writes as one who finds in some of the central events of the Christian narrative — the Garden of Eden, the Crucifixion, the atonement of Mary Magdalene — a powerful statement of his view of the human condition and a powerful drama that he can adapt, as he continually adapted

is one of the deadly sins.
We must detach ourselves
by playfulness. The
man who murders is
undoubtedly a great
sinner. But the man
who becomes virtuous
in the ordinary sense,
is worse than a murderer.

It is here that rests the
structure of Cockcrow. To
present it as truth, as
serious truth, w'd be
wrong. It can only be
presented as play to
the mind.

Thoreau's observation, about
never working. But only
playing.

Cockcrow's evolution
is this. How terrible
is the picture of the
Hindu saint, with his
fierce drive to destroy
his ego. But let
him play, and the
ego goes.

The terrible thing about
modern man is not
that he is without art—
but that his art is such
a desperate preoccupation.
The garden of Eden
playfulness is gone.
He is a serious artist.
Everyone talks about
self-expression. Everyone
is the thing which he is
not.

". . . only playing"
(91-20)

Shakespeare's plots, to his own symbolic and allegorical ends. In his drama, figures such as Cockcrow and Gramsci stand in for what he understood as the major dilemmas of contemporary humanity. They also stand in for the artist: for what Watson understood as the artist's self-sacrifice, capacity to transfigure through art, and movement toward redemption though a co-creation of artist, actor, and spectator/reader.

If one writes from within the Christian allegory, this raises the question of whether the artist usurps the role of God, a question Watson asked himself many times during the 1950s. He found his salvation from Satanic hubris in the "playfulness" of *Cockcrow*. "I think of the Tree of Good and Evil as being the Tree of Art. . . . sin is essentially, being more God-like than the degree of being permits," he reflected:

Above all, the Xn must avoid those sins which remove him from God, by making him God's competitor. Seriousness in anything, is one of the deadly sins. We must detach ourselves by playfulness. . . .

It is here that rests the structure of Cockcrow. To present it as truth, as serious truth, wd be wrong. It can only be presented as play to the mind. . . . (91-20 Jan 28 1958)

Outline of revisions to *Cockcrow*, May 1958 (91-24)

With a renewed commitment to an existential playfulness, and no doubt seriously encouraged by a conversation in which Gordon Peacock had spoken of wanting to stage new Canadian plays (SW-514[5] WW to SW Feb 16 [1958]), Watson turned to the task of making *Cockcrow* stageworthy.

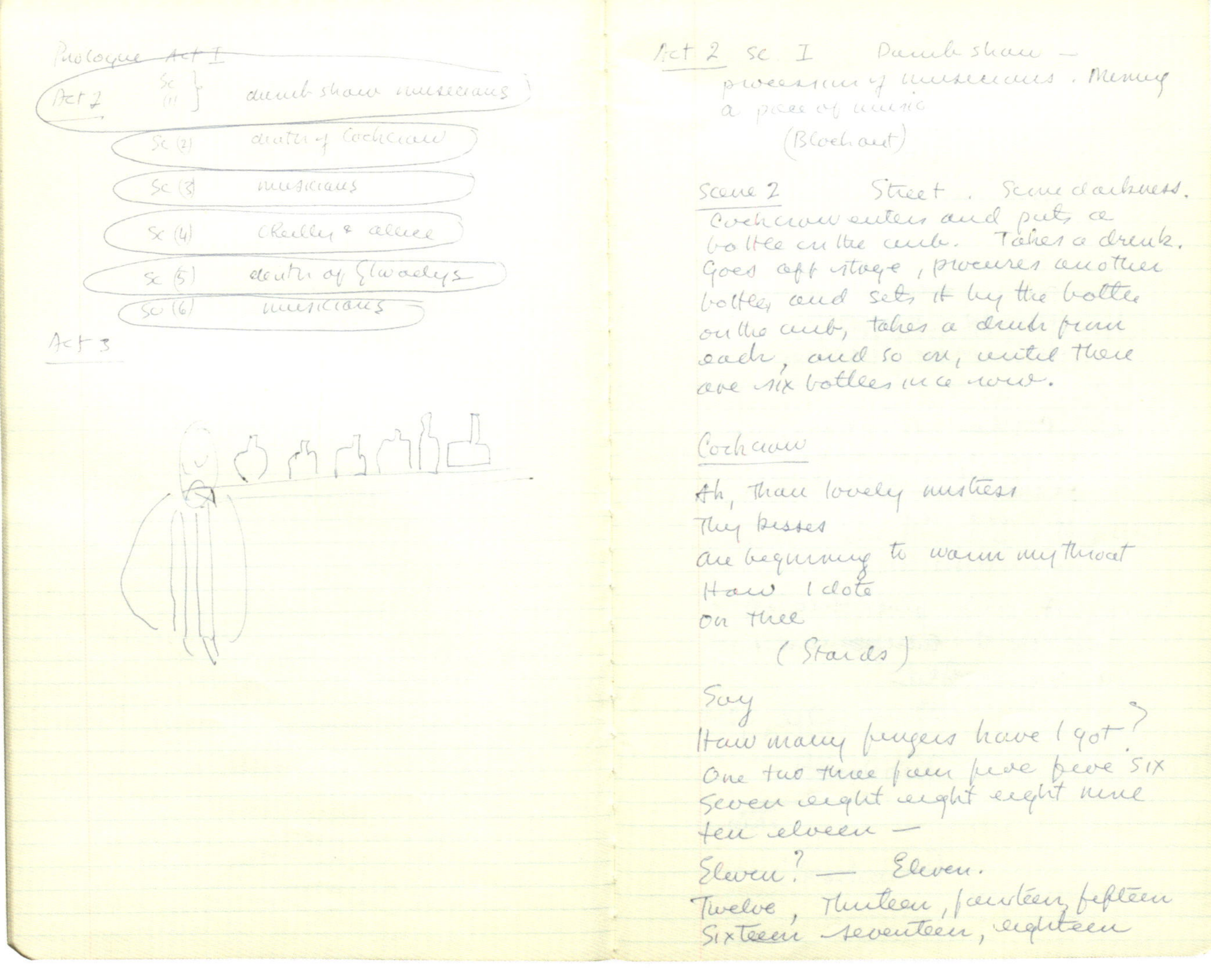
~~Prologue Act I~~
Act 2 Sc (1) } dumb show musicians
Sc (2) death of Cockcrow
Sc (3) musicians
Sc (4) O'Reilly & Alice
Sc (5) death of Gladys
Sc (6) musicians
Act 3

Act 2 Sc. I Dumb show — procession of musicians.

Scene 2 Street. Some darkness.
Cockcrow enters and puts a bottle on the curb. Takes a drink. Goes off stage, procures another bottle and sets it by the bottle on the curb, takes a drink from each, and so on, until there are six bottles in a row.

Cockcrow

Ah, thou lovely mistress
Thy kisses
are beginning to warm my throat
How I dote
on thee
(Stands)

Say
How many fingers have I got?
One two three four five five six
Seven eight eight eight nine
ten eleven —
Eleven? — Eleven.
Twelve, thirteen, fourteen, fifteen
Sixteen seventeen, eighteen

In his 1958 revision he focused less on plot and action than he had in the past, and more on shortcomings, on development, on structure, on patterns. In May, he made a list of the work to be done on the play and noted that he had a "very tentative" new beginning that made the character of Pride more meaningful (91-24 May 16 1958). A good deal of his journal commentary is given to clarifying the conflicts between his characters and the turning points within and between each of them over the course of the play. He struggled to bring together his three themes: the "Cockcrow and revelation theme," the "attraction/repulsion theme of O'Reilly/Alice" or "love," and the "King/murderer theme of Higgins," or "politics" (91-25).

Perhaps as a consequence of his intensive theatre going in Paris, he began to think in terms of production. He imagined how the musicians' score could be a kind of mime (91-55) and how stage blocking could create "a wrenching of attention" from "major action" to "distraction action" (91-25 Aug 21 1958). He thought a good deal about pacing. In late August the conclusion of the first act troubled him and led to a comparison to

Facing page:
Watson's drawing for the "dumbshow" of Cockcrow on the curb with his bottles (91-55)

Ionesco: "This is partly an *accablement* of phrases — resembling the conclusion of *The Bald Soprano*, but with meaningful rather than unmeaningful phrase" (Aug 25 1991). In early September, he assessed the "complexity" of the third act and concluded, "There is nothing in Shakespeare so complex. Yet the complexity is unavoidable, and it is integrated" (91-26 Sept 3 1958). "To redeem the delay and length" of Act III, he decided that he would need in the last acts "to move with great swiftness" (Sept 8 1958).

During this round of revision, Watson developed and theorized four dramatic techniques that he would use throughout his career as a playwright: submergence, enacted imagery, root actions, and vectors. He took the concept of submergence from Gabriel Marcel and articulated it as a dramatic technique when he changed Higgins's trade from barber to ironmonger so that his Canadian Cockney aspirant to political office might declare, "I shall have nothing more to do with nails" (91-25 Aug 23 1958; *Plays* 33). In the play's Crucifixion scene when, ever the embodiment of scientific rationalism, Higgins refuses to drive a nail, the "emergent" feeling of the later scene returns us to our "submerged participation" in that feeling in the earlier statement (Marcel, I.114). "Submergence," Watson told himself, was "a kind of restraint" and an important way of ensuring the audience's *co-creation* of the play:

> The meaning is submerged beneath all the means of expression, imagery, ideas etc.
>
> It is an ironic, as well as allegoric quality. . . .
>
> Realism is the great enemy of submergence. Because it implies a stated meaning, whereas the submerged style states an implication. If it be true, as I think, that an author, from the beginning, starts as a co-author, submergence is a quality which permits his collaborators to do their work easily. (91-20 Feb 16 1958)

In Watson's experience, this "subliminal organization" was "peculiar to poetry" (91-33 Mar 12 1960). It was one of the reasons he wanted to write not drama, but verse drama.

Facing page: "The Nativity"; Watson drew this image for the last act of *Cockcrow* many times in his 1958 notebooks (91-55)

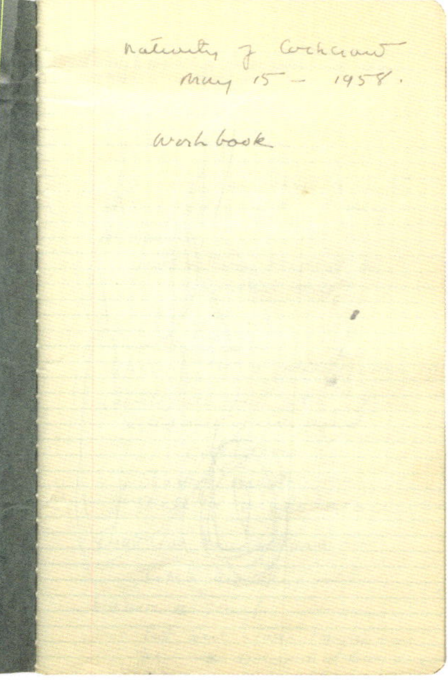

He decided that "the proper imagery of a play is in its enacted images": "E.g. Cockcrow/Pot of Geraniums/Dressing of Pride/The lashing of Cyril/The crucifying. . . ." (91-55). Enacted images such as Cockcrow's bottles, Cyril's whip, the rope, and the pearl bear an increased weight of meaning as his drafts succeed one another. In an outline for a "Preface to Cockcrow" he was explicit about enacted imagery: "the pot of geraniums, Queenie's kiss, and the pearl are not allegories for love as 'giving,' but allegories which explore giving as a way of expressing love, where giving can entail binding, or contempt, or release from remorse" (91-72). Like gesture, enacted images create meaning by virtue of their tension with the spoken word.

The concept of "root actions," or actions that lead "to an obligatory scene," enabled him to think through the relation of dramatic structure to dramatic action. He examined the tightness of his plot, for example, by analyzing its root actions: thus "Cyril's accusation of his father" is a root action that "necessitates the trial," that "necessitates the scarecrow crucifixion," that necessitates the despair of O'Reilly and Cockcrow, that "necessitates the Pearl scene," that "necessitates the nativity." And so on for Cockcrow's vow, and Alice's rejection of O'Reilly (91-469).

He also began to think about dramatic action in terms of "moment" and "vector." "The power of drama," he reminded himself, "lies in the moment."

> But the temporal condition requires movement from moment to moment and this is achieved by what could be called vectors. . . .
>
> The vector is the enemy.
>
> . . . Medieval drama (based on scripture, and the Stations of the Cross) uses moment & vector more successfully than any other drama that I know.
>
> The moment is given its full extent. Then a swift economical vector passage places the action at the next moment. (91-24 May 26 1958)

Almost twenty-five years later, writing *Gramsci x 3*, a Passion play, based on the Stations of the Cross, he will note once again that "I build a play by a vector/target system" (91-296 Nov 13 1982).

… the long apprenticeship completed: Final revisions to Cockcrow

IN MID-AUGUST 1958 Watson began "what seems a very final draft" (91-25 Aug 18 1958). The draft he completed in October would run, he estimated, two hours and forty-eight minutes. He had excised much of the Masque of the City (although the Carnival of the Animals remained), had written a good deal of new dialogue, and had tightened the play immeasurably. In December, he had the manuscript typed and began to think about the next revision. In January 1959 he resumed revisions, working from the new typescript. He imagined the release from despair of O'Reilly and Cockcrow "as generating a babble" and a "chorus-like, Agnus dei" (Jan 1 1959), which is how the play does end. In order to "enact" his images, he decided that O'Reilly would spit on the scarecrow and the spit would become the pearl (Jan 9 1959). In late May, he contemplated "an abbreviated Cockcrow" (91-29 May 31 1959) and provided an outline

An "abbreviated Cockcrow," May 1959 (91-29)

Abbreviated Cockcrow

I The vow
(a) Cyril & the heralds
(b) Higgins and Cockcrow
(c) The vow *

II death of Gladys
(a) the drawing of Cockcrow
(b) Cyril & his mother
(c) quarrel of Alice & O'Reilly (abbreviated)
(d) death of Gladys Higgins *

III Return of Cockcrow
(a) O'Reilly reports Cockcrow's death
(b) return of Cockcrow
(c) entrance of Boswell (very brief)
(d) drunken dance
(e) death of Higgins *

IV Trial
V Crucifixion of Scarecrow
VI despair
VII Rescue.

* climaxes

Principally, a subordination of the Alice/O'Reilly parts & the narrative of Cockcrow & Boswell of the play. In most respects that outline is the play as we have it: the Masque of the City of the Dead and the Carnival of the Animals have been entirely suppressed, and the scenes follow the order we know.

There are several typescripts of *Cockcrow* in the archive: one likely dates from the 1958 version of the manuscript; another is probably from the 1959 revision; the others are certainly from the 1960 and 1961 versions. They can perhaps be dated by their titles: the earliest ones are called "A Vision of Cockcrow," suggesting just how late in the compositional process Watson relinquished the idea of framing the play as a "dream" or "vision." Others are called *Cockcrow and the Gulls,* a title Watson arrived at only in October 1960. All have manuscript emendations, sometimes extensive. They offer rich material for a textual study of the development of the play.

On June 2, 1959, Watson recorded starting the outlined revision, which he judged "very rough in texture" but successful in having reduced the playing time to two hours. In July he introduced a crucial new scene, the madness of Alice. It addressed a need for an image to express the state of mind of the women after the Crucifixion scene, and it provided him with a chiasmus from the "defeat," the "mixed horror and bliss," of the first four acts of the play to the "togetherness-redemption" of the last act (91-30 July 16 1959; 91-25 July 9 1959). He also offered his clearest statement of the *Measure for Measure* theme, as it informs the scenes of the trial and Crucifixion: "sin entails the sin of punishment" (91-25 July 25 1959). It is at this point that he made his unsuccessful submission of the play to Coach House Press.

In October 1960, Watson turned to "infinitesimal revision" of the play (91-40 Oct 10 1960). The brothel-owner Mother Manning became Mother Loving. He drafted wordy prologues for the character of Pride, before replacing these with additional dialogue in which Pride declares himself a musician and, therefore, a physician. In April 1961, he considered a few further revisions, most notably his introduction of what he called "the Virgil-technique": "quotation from / Shakespeare / Wyatt / Bacon / Yeats / Chaucer." No reader or viewer of *Cockcrow* can fail to miss these, particularly near the beginning of the play. "The theory is," Watson explained, "that these interpolations represent the public consciousness" and "that they provide a platform from which the descent into drama is made" (91-62 April 22 1961). And in August he had a further thought on the intersubjectivity of playwright and audience: "Gulls — the audience? In Shakespeare, the audience are witnesses. But here the audience becomes an accomplice" (91-66 Aug 1 1961).

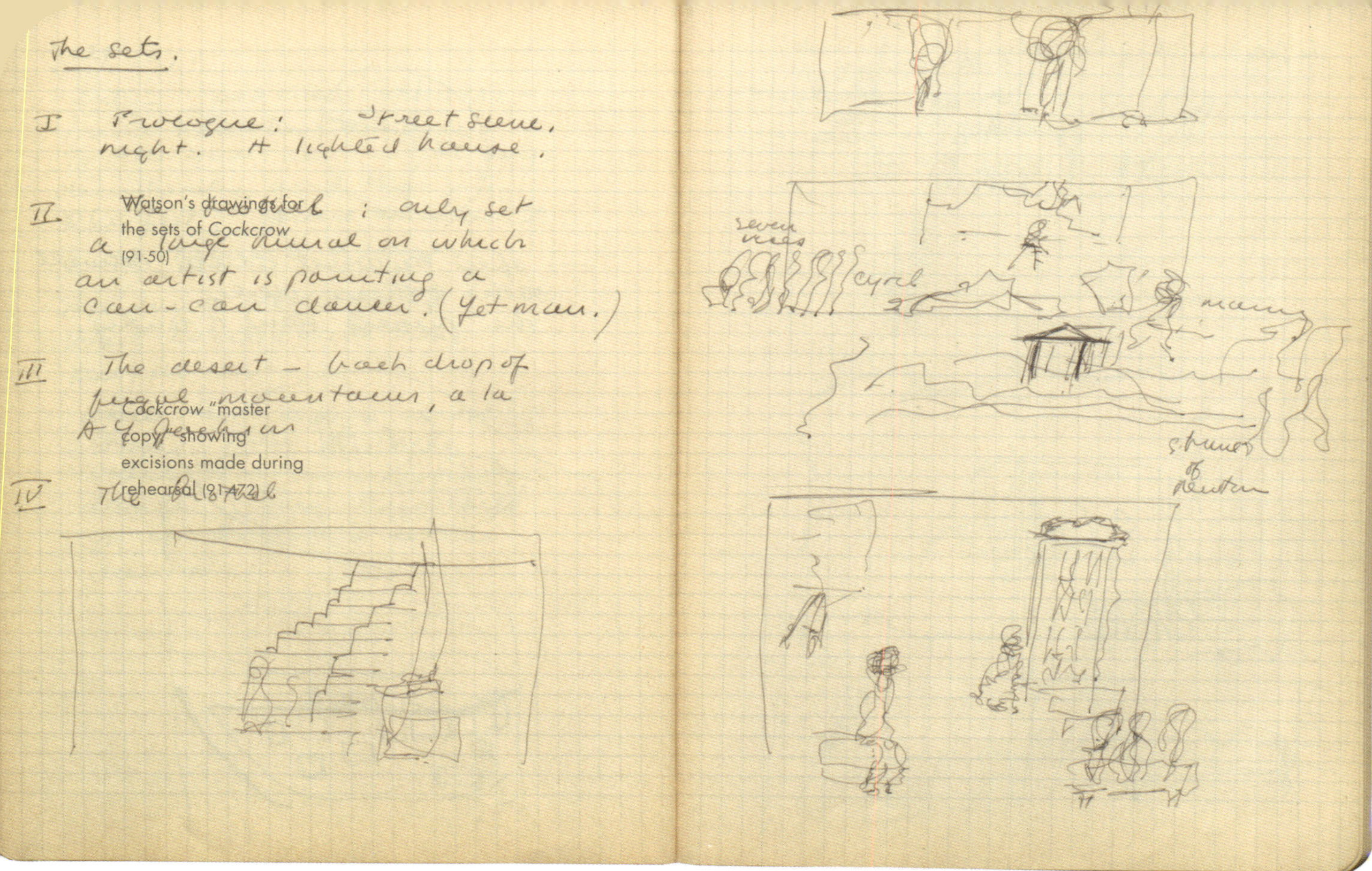

the sets.
I Prologue: Street scene, night. A lighted house.
an artist is painting a can-can dancer.
III The desert – back drop of

Watson's drawings for the sets of *Cockcrow* (91-50)

Facing page: *Cockcrow* "master copy," showing excisions made during rehearsal (91-472)

This revision is, in all likelihood, the one Watson bound and gave to Gordon Peacock for production. And now the play underwent one last ruthless round of revisions (91-472). This typescript, which contains handwritten names of cast and crew, has passage after passage crossed out. Scarce one in two pages escapes excisions. It bears the closest scrutiny for it can tell us how the process of working with a production team — his "own troupe" — enabled Watson further to sharpen further the dialogue and action of the play, and it can tell us how closely Watson, Peacock, and the actors collaborated during rehearsals.

What had his fourteen-year apprenticeship writing *Cockcrow and the Gulls* taught Watson? Observing how he shapes the fecundity and complexity of his ideas in order to write a stage-worthy play, we see him mastering a range of dramatic techniques: learning what to keep and what to discard; learning how to translate ideas into dialogue, gesture, stage properties, and enacted images; and learning how to create meaning out of the tensions among them. He learned how to write colloquial speech, from O'Reilly's "Irish" clichés to Higgins's Cockney to Iris's garrulousness, in verse. Convinced that

3-40

COCKCROW AND THE GULLS

act one

SCENE ONE: semi-darkness. Nanaimo. At night. A street of brothels. In front of Mother Loving's house. Pride, maestro of a second-rate jazz orchestra of some local reputation, struts in. He is carrying violin and violin-case. He puts the instrument into its case. A moment later, enter Thomas Higgin's boy, Cyril. He escorts a pot of red geraniums. He doesn't see Pride, but looks up and down the darkness of the street, as if seeking an address.

PRIDE. Sweetly though ~~(with a good show of lung)~~

~~Holoa there. Holoa holoa there.~~
~~For shame,~~
~~Say,~~
~~Have you lost your way?~~

~~(to audience)~~

Regard the pot of geraniums.
~~Regard the sunny of the pot of geraniums.~~
May
I, before this ~~play~~ ~~comedy~~ play
Deviates any further into allegory,
Introduce to you the owner of the pot of geraniums?
He is one Cyril Higgins

(mimicking the boy)

~~The kid cocks his head pure robin~~
~~Red-breasted with a pot of -- what colour are they? --~~
~~pink ger-rye-ne-ums~~
~~(prances)~~

~~How'm I doing?~~

~~(confidentially)~~

~~A psychologist's mixed-up teenager certainly.~~
He is looking for his father.
So I gather. A queer kid.
As for me -- you all know me, my Christian name is...Pride.
~~I am your self-respect, and though a musician~~
My mother was a Christian gentlewoman.
I was most religiously begotten.
She baptized me, Pride.
Here endeth my aside.

(to Cyril)

Whoring, Cyril Higgins?
O god...hasn't the human race...any self-respect?

~~(...)~~

Have you lost your way, yes?

CYRIL. (stutters and stammers)

I was l-looking f-for an a-a-address.
Wh-what h-house is th-this?

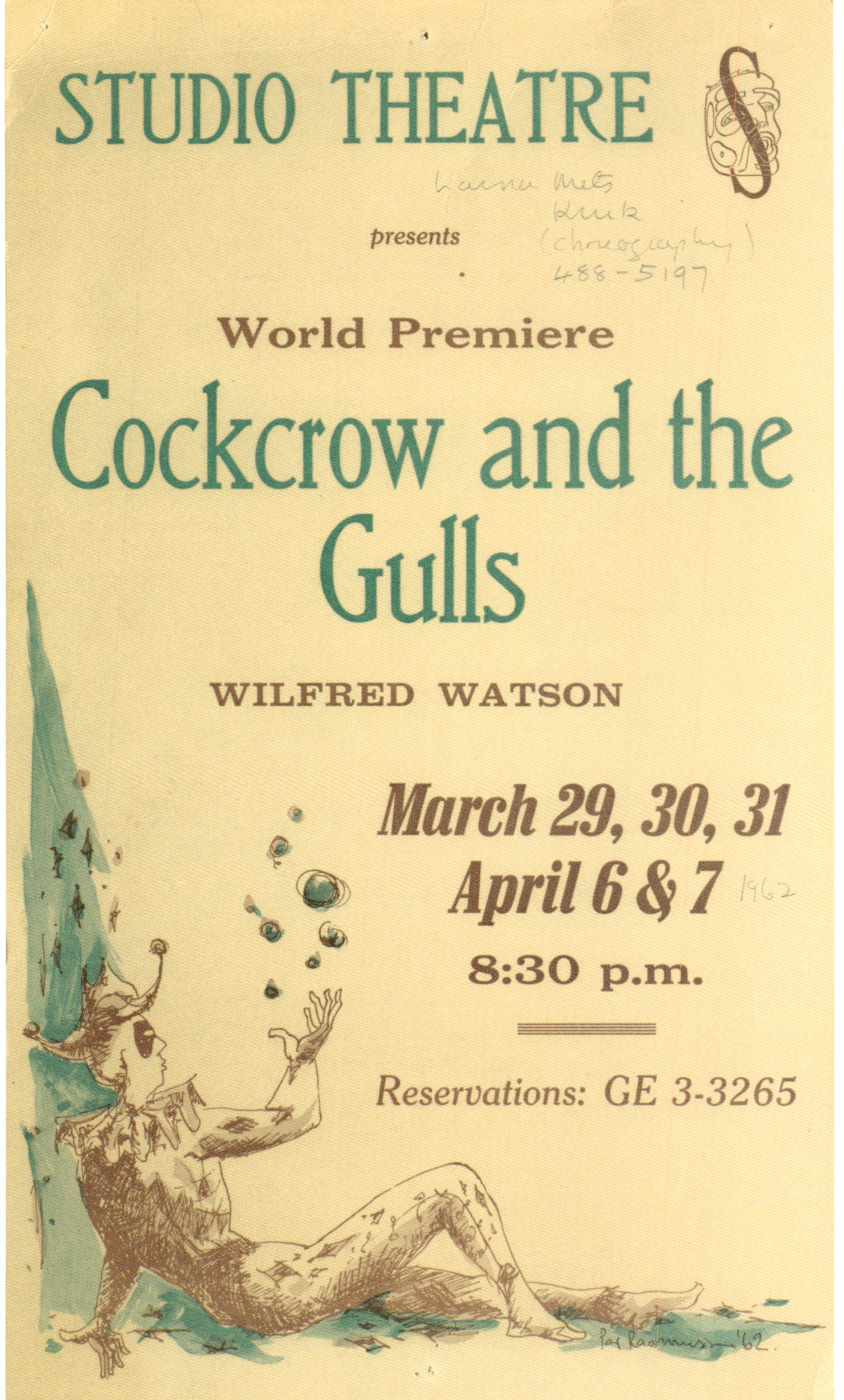

Poster announcing *Cockcrow and the Gulls* (95-641)

Facing page:
"We . . . we've got some crucifying to do": Act four, scene five of *Cockcrow and the Gulls*, Studio Theatre, 1962 (95-24-54)

"drama can present material so complex that it is not capable of being arranged in narrative form . . . and should do so" (91-72), he learned how to create meaning by means of "submergence," by means of emblematic stage properties, and most importantly, by means of ritual. He learned how, with complex ideas, "allegory can be used as a method of exploration, and that this sort of reconnaissance-allegory is more dramatic than the didactic allegory of Spenser and Bunyan" (*Ibid*). He learned how to avoid didacticism by embracing playfulness. He learned how to structure his drama so as to create bridges within the play from tragic farce to "togetherness-redemption," and he learned "that dramatic art, indeed all art, must create a bridge between man's vanished beliefs, and his contemporary unbelief" (*Ibid*). In a noteworthy repudiation of the egocentrism of the Romantic (or the Modernist) subjectivity of the artist, he learned to understand the work of art as a co-creation between playwright, director, actor, and audience, between poet and reader. That learning entailed much "unlearning."

Previous spread: On May 22 1966, in the notebook in which this image appears, Watson writes: "I came in the last few months to know what theatre of the absurd was about. It is about two things: clichés; obstacles. The cliché is the most human, the most highly significant part of language. The obstacle. This is the limit of a medium, the extent of an extension of man." (91-127).

Facing page: Watson's painting opposite a journal entry from early September 1964: "Theater of the absurd is haunted by time, because 17th cent murdered time. 20thC murdered space." (91-101)

Unlearning . . . Decolonizing

Watson entered the 1960s having heeded criticisms that poems in *Friday's Child* were derivative of the Modernists and that he had not found his own voice: his journals through the late 1950s include several assessments of what he had achieved or failed to achieve with that collection. Retrospectively he would claim that following its publication, "I consciously attempted to follow Ezra Pound & unlearn what I'd learned from the poets of the Roberts Faber Book of Modern Verse, which started with an anachronistic inclusion of G.M. Hopkins and end[ed] with one or two lyrics by Dylan Thomas." He described "the unlearning process" as "almost completed" with the writing, in 1959, of "A Manifesto for Beast Poetry" and wryly noted that "I was then aged 48, a rather late age to start a new career" (91-252 Feb 19 1981).

Some of his "unlearning" was about form: he writes "A Manifesto" in a straightforward syntax and in very loose iambic metre that mixes short and long lines (what he called "biphrasals"). Some of it was enabled by his systematic reading of the works of Wyndham Lewis beginning in late 1955 and intensifying after Sheila Watson began her Ph.D. research on that writer. Lewis provided lessons to both the Watsons about how to remove "point of view" and narrator interventions from their writing. Watson was particularly

Contents
(1) The trumpet as an extension of man
(2) The porcupine quill
nostalgia for bushpilots
(3) Bushpilots are romantic
(4) Love in the cold night of montreal
(5) As I walked down

"Extensions of man," Oct 5–Nov 15 1964 notebook (91-105).

drawn to Lewis's notions that our minds are altered by their extensions (an idea he also found in McLuhan) and that comedy occurs when men behave like machines. But most of his "unlearning" focused on the question of what it meant to be a Canadian writer writing Canadian literature. The orthodoxy of his time, which held that Canadian literature was written by Canadians and somehow expressed a Canadian "identity," was anathema to Watson. He decried even more the concept of regionalism. For Watson, "the distinguishing feature of permanent literature" was the "matching of form and content" (91-237 May 13 1979). He did not believe that a writer could create a Canadian literature by pouring new content into traditional forms borrowed from English verse or into *vers libre* borrowed from American poets. The result of doing so, he observed, was that "The salmon was Canadian alright but the can wasn't" (91-240 Apr 6 1980). He understood his "unlearning" as "an agonizing shift from the colonial, colonized and colonizing, poet of Friday's Child," indebted to English verse traditions, "to a Canadianist." The difficulty lay in making the shift "without becoming an American re-colonized colonial" (*Ibid*), that is, in finding an indigenous form. "A Manifesto" is savagely satirical about the Canadian literary culture of its time and it ends with a "call out aloud to the future / . . . to cut itself off boldly from all its ancestors" and from "the free & easy verse opinions" (*Poems* 56).

Watson struggled over the next years to find a new form for the literature of a newish nation. His first sustained collection to throw off the traditional forms of English verse while avoiding American *vers libre* was "A Bawl of Wool," poems written from behind the mask of "Jenny Blake," a decidedly embodied anima figure who often speaks in short, spiky lines in which rhyme yields to assonance.[24] The persona of "Jenny" was one of several attempts by Watson in the 1960s to "synthesize my development in verse and my experiments in theatre" (91-252 Feb 19 1981). He felt he had made a breakthrough in this synthesis with "I shot a trumpet into my brain," written in 1962-63, the first of the poems collected in *The Sorrowful Canadians,* and a poem that he would describe as a "formal articulation" of his belief in "the Lewisian/McLuhan recognition that the human mind is modified by its extensions" (91-281 draft letter to Doreen Watt Nov 19 1981):

> **I shot a trumpet into my brain**
> My left eye became a telescope.
> **I shot a trumpet into my brain**
> my blasted eye-socket suffered a sea-change.
> **I shot a trumpet into my brain**
> and by a conversion became a navigator's sextant.
> **I shot a trumpet into my brain**
> through a fragment of bone I saw the new moon. (*Poems* 148)

The repeated line functions a little like the refrain of a ballad, creating a rhythm by means of regularly restating an action. More importantly for Watson, it lifts the words off the page; they are almost impossible to read without wishing to chant them. There is something, too, of call and response between the repeated line and the "filling" between its iterations. Watson had begun to move his poetry off the page and into performance.

With this poem, he judged himself successful in another way, one tied implicitly to McLuhan's *The Mechanical Bride* and explicitly to a perceived failing in *Friday's Child*: "One of the criticisms of FC I took to heart was the lack of (what Madison Square admen called) product recognition." With "I shot a trumpet into my brain," he later wrote,

> I achieved (I felt) product recognition. The subject matter = McLuhan. The form was W.W. I adapted the form from Garcia Lorca's Death of the Bull Fighter, which I saw in Roy Campbell's translation: by keeping the repeated line like the crack of a whip, but using the sandwich filling with prose-like freedom.[25] This form I worked all through the sixties. (91-252 Feb 19 1981)

The "product" toward which he was moving was not only one labelled "W.W." In creating a new form, into which to pour his new wine, Watson had taken the first step he believed necessary to creating "a permanent literature," one he was willing to call Canadian.

Facing page:
Theatre program for *O Holy Ghost, DIP YOUR FINGER IN THE BLOOD OF CANADA, and write, I LOVE YOU,* Studio Theatre, 1962 (95-639)

"A Small Theatre Group"

In "The Canadian Fact," a one-act play that opened at Walterdale Playhouse on May 26, 1967, a Canadian writer, who may or may not write Canadian plays, engages in an absurdist dialogue with a Canadian director who has never directed a Canadian play. Set in "any Canadian theatre . . . not so much a scene, as a fascinating but devastating sense of the totally foreign, of the place furthest removed from home," the play begins *in medias res*:

> the first thing a Canadian writer feels when he goes into a Canadian theatre is a marked hostility. . . . it is so, I assure you. I am a writer, and that is what I feel. . . . A Canadian writer is definitely not, N,O,T, not welcome in a Canadian theatre. (53)[26]

Walterdale Theatre Associates (originally Edmonton Theatre Associates) was an amateur group founded in August 1958; "The Canadian Fact," a Centennial-year offering directed by Peter Montgomery, was one of two Watson plays staged there. (The other was *Two Teardrops Frozen on a Rearview Mirror* directed by Joan Krisch.)

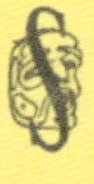

the drama department of the university of alberta has been commissioned by the edmonton civic centennial committee to produce

Oh Holy Ghost DIP YOUR FINGER IN THE BLOOD OF CANADA and write, I LOVE YOU

an original
FLOWER-POWER-FARCE
by

Wilfred Watson *writer*
& Thomas Peacocke *director*
& Leonard Feldman *designer*
& Anne Burrows *music*
& Alice and Phil Switzer *graphics*

&

Alexander Diakun *Richard Sunflower & avatars*
& Jay Smith *Pinkie Green & avatars*
& Paul Letourneau *Roger Sunflower & avatars*
& Elmer Hohol *Robert Sunflower & avatars*
& Pieternella Versloot *Sappho Sunflower & avatars*
& Catherine Jackson *Helen Yort & avatars*
& Linda Kupecek *Katerina & avatars*
& Nancy Beatty *Ariadne & avatars*
& Carole Harmon *Puce & avatars*

& Dave McCulley	*Stage Manager*
& Pamela Ormston	*1st Assistant Stage Manager*
& Carole Harmon	*2nd Assistant Stage Manager*
& Kurt Grieser	*Photographer*
& Peter Kirchmeir	*Technical Assistant, Sets*
& Ron East	*Sets*
& Dennis Simpson	*Shop Carpenter*
& Axel Peterson	*Shop Carpenter*
& June Emery	*Costume Cutter*
& Linda Rabinovitch	*Costume Crew*
& Dieter Wessels	*Technical Assistant, Lights*
& John Holland	*Lights*
& William Riske	*Lights*
& George Jendyk	*Sound*
& Norval Loney	*Property Master*
& Kathy Scheelar	*Projectionist*
& Omaya al Karmy	*Projectionist*
& Peter Mueller	*Stage Crew*
& Candace Oliver	*Stage Crew*
& Pat Flood	*Stage Crew*
& Carol Lazare	*Stage Crew*
& Jack Winterton	*Business Manager*
& Cathy Lakin	*House Manager*
& Peter Emery	*Program*

& YOU

& we acknowledge . . .

Music Department + University of Toronto
C.B.X.T. + Dr. J. D. M. Alton
Harry Beleshko of the Windsor Wig Centre
CFRN-TV + Edmonton Journal
CKUA-radio + the Gateway
Chris Rideout

&

REMEMBER

Due to the current production of THE BIRTHDAY PARTY in New York, we are not permitted to produce Pinter's play, in February. In its place we will present Samuel Beckett's tragi-comedy, WAITING FOR GODOT, February 6th to 10th. All patrons will receive selection cards in January.

In "The Canadian Fact," Writer and Director together develop an "oral playscript" with the working title "AMERICAN BOMBARDMENT OF A LUNATIC ASYLUM IN HANOI WHILE PETER BROOK WAS DIRECTING A CANADIAN TELEPHONE DIRECTORY THERE." In the midst of creating the play, the Director suddenly feels proud he is a Canadian and proposes they sing "O Canada" together. After they sing, however, the Director remarks: "But having discovered that I am a Canadian, I find myself beginning to question your script . . . (pause) which was the cause of my realizing a true sense of Canadian identity." What, he asks, "has a script about Peter Brook in a lunatic asylum in Hanoi to do with myself and my fellow Canadians in Canada?"

DIRECTOR	. . . [I]s it really a Canadian play?
WRITER	Well, I am a Canadian. How could I write anything but a Canadian play? (pause) The lunatic asylum is a metaphor for Canada. (pause) Peter Brook is a metaphor for the Canadian theatre. (pause) The Canadian telephone directory is a metaphor for the Canadian people. (62)

Watson satirizes both the cultural nationalism of the day and the state of theatre in Canada. "The Canadian Fact" had a second run at the Walterdale in October 1967. Weeks later, another Watson Centennial offering, *O Holy Ghost, DIP YOUR FINGER IN THE BLOOD OF CANADA and write, I LOVE YOU*, directed by Thomas Peacocke, opened at Studio Theatre.

Unlike the Writer in "The Canadian Fact," by the early 1960s Watson had begun finding directors willing to produce his plays. He had found his small theatre group in the Alumni Studio A Players under the direction of Gordon Peacock. Peacock had ambitious plans for both a BFA in Drama and for Studio Theatre; increasingly he involved Watson. The turning point in Watson's involvement with Studio Theatre was Peacock's decision to produce *Cockcrow and the Gulls* and to make Watson's play the capstone of Studio Theatre's 1961–62 season. Peacock opened the production on March 29, 1962, its run planned to coincide with the Western Canadian Educational Theatre Conference on "New Directions in Theatre" (April 6–8 1962). Prominent American as well as Canadian theatre directors, critics, and media representatives attended the conference, and the première of *Cockcrow* received national coverage.[27]

was teleological not
causal.

Gordon Peacock

His directing was
not authoritarian
but charismatic.
He thought of
the actors as
revolutionaries, not
as inmates of a
brothel selling their
bodies for the pleasure
of the audience. He
came to the audience
as if it were the
Supreme Court
of Canada and
passed judgment
on it. His theatre

Watson on Gordon Peacock's directing, recollected while preparing *Plays at the Iron Bridge* (95-130)

Left:
Cockcrow and the Gulls theatre program cover, reproducing Norman Yates' study for the set design (95-639)

Below:
Cockcrow and the Gulls theatre program (95-639)

PROLOGUE

***Moon-Parrots of Nanaimo**

You must not think
That the moon-parrots
Of Nanaimo are
The blathering swans
Of the mud tongue
Of the river of
Every will be done
As you won't be
Come by, or that the
Coal of the harbour
Like Isaiah's fire
Will blench the breath
Or whiten the teeth
Of every jaw of rock
Our ship of fools till
Cockcrow shall sail by;
Or that every stone
Which sinks down
To the bottom of the ocean,
Crying, Lord, Lord, Lord, shall drown.

for G.P.

*re-named, **Cockcrow and the Gulls**

-:- -:- -:- -:- -:-

Cockcrow and the Gulls

It was exciting several months ago to read **Cockcrow and the Gulls** for the first time. It has been a privilege in preparing for performance a play that has such a deeply moving spiritual quality. Its all there, an intense theatricalism, a distance from reality, and the spectators consciousness of a universe in which he may or may not participate.

Wilfred Watson is a poet, and it is not the function of the poet to clarify. **Cockcrow and the Gulls** requires a dual state of consciousness in the spectator, who at once believes and disbelieves. A statement from us on what we believe the meaning of the play to be would be wrong, as a spectator's involvement should be an individual one.

Having the playwright on the scene during rehearsals, especially one with such a deep understanding of theatrical problems, is greatly appreciated.

G.P.

-:- -:- -:- -:- -:-

The Poet in the Theatre

" . . . I start with the assumption that if poetry is merely a decoration, an added embellishment, if it merely gives people of literary tastes the pleasure of listening to poetry at the same time that they are witnessing a play, then it is superfluous. It must justify itself dramatically, and not merely be fine poetry shaped into dramatic form. From this it follows that no play should be written in verse for which prose is dramatically adequate."

T. S. Eliot

" . . . drama, after all, is not life, but like all art, an abstraction from life. The characters are not, in any biological sense, independent organisms, but, within the limits of work of art which is the limit of their existence, simply marionettes of abstraction, symbols of the literary pattern."

Raymond Williams

Studio Theatre Players

present

THE WORLD PREMIERE OF

COCKCROW AND THE GULLS

Wilfred Watson

Cast in order of Appearance

Five Musicians:		Cockcrow	Hutchison Shandro
Pride	Robert Mumford	Gwladys Higgins	Betty Evans
Wrath	Bud D'Amur	Angel	Kay Martin
Sloth	Donald Wells	First Pedestrian	Wes Cummings
Envy	Gordon Zard	Second Pedestrian	Ian Heacock
Nunsclip Lechery	Beverley Barnhouse	Third Pedestrian	Lee Royce
Cyril	Bernard Havard	Iris	Sylvia Shore
Higgins	Kenneth Welsh	Boswell	Thomas Peacocke
Queenie	Esther Norville	Dancers and Strangers	Wes Cummings
Alice	Sheila Daniels		Ian Heacock
Greta	Louise Wood		Norman Pettersson
O'Reilly	Garry Mitchell		
Mother Loving	Jean Craig	Logger-Shepherd	Norman Pettersson

Time: The Present

Act I: Nanaimo

Act II: A Place

Directed by Gordon Peacock

Designed by Norman Yates

(Coffee will be available in the main lobby during intermission.)

The exhibition of painting in the Lobby is from the work of Norman Yates, Dipartment of Fine Arts

PRODUCTION STAFF

Technical Director	Frank Bueckert	Costumes	Melissa Matkin
Technical Assistant	Robert Mumford		Shirley Howard
Assistant Director	Lee Royce	Properties	Muriel Johnson
Stage Manager	Kay Martin		Linda Frame
Assistant Stage Manager	Wes Cummings	Lighting	Peter Burns
Music arranged by	Anne Burrows		Karen Austin
Set Construction	Kenneth Smith		Irene Bergen
	Richard Swaren	Sound	Torrey Crozier
	Elsie Zaychowski		Alexander Diakun
	Grania Daly	Publicity and Promotion	Dorothy Clark
	Elaine Verchomin	House Manager	Marion Trainor
	Kenneth Welsh	Ushers	Student Nurses, U.A.H.
	Class of Drama 250		Drama Division Students
		Seamstress	Ruth Wosic

ACKNOWLEDGMENTS

CKUA, CHED, CFRN, CHFA, CJCA, CFRN-TV, CBXT
The Edmonton Journal
Harmony Kids
Anne Pettersson
Sheila Hunchak
Caretaking Staff, Education Building

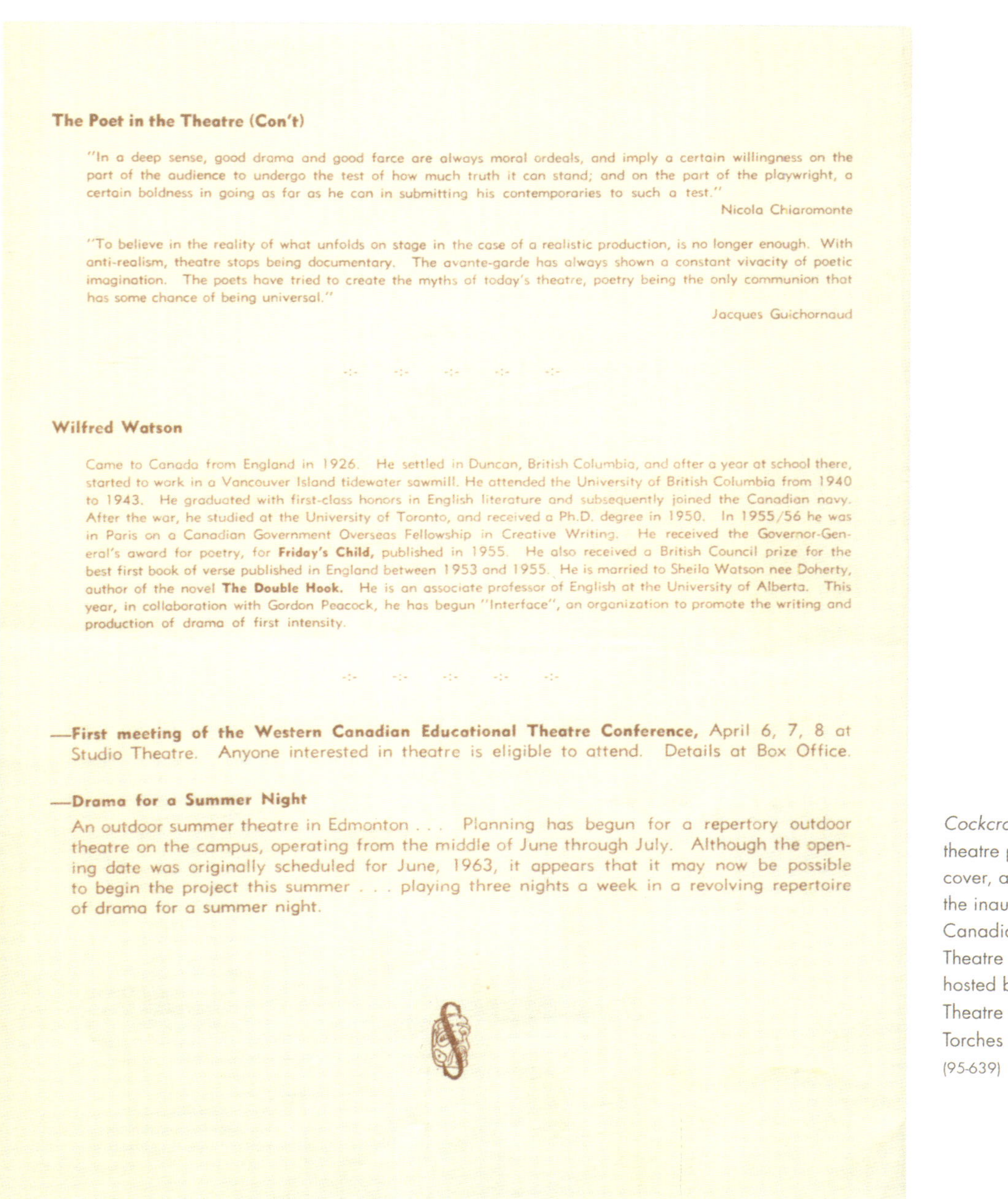

The Poet in the Theatre (Con't)

"In a deep sense, good drama and good farce are always moral ordeals, and imply a certain willingness on the part of the audience to undergo the test of how much truth it can stand; and on the part of the playwright, a certain boldness in going as far as he can in submitting his contemporaries to such a test."

Nicola Chiaromonte

"To believe in the reality of what unfolds on stage in the case of a realistic production, is no longer enough. With anti-realism, theatre stops being documentary. The avante-garde has always shown a constant vivacity of poetic imagination. The poets have tried to create the myths of today's theatre, poetry being the only communion that has some chance of being universal."

Jacques Guichornaud

-:- -:- -:- -:- -:-

Wilfred Watson

Came to Canada from England in 1926. He settled in Duncan, British Columbia, and after a year at school there, started to work in a Vancouver Island tidewater sawmill. He attended the University of British Columbia from 1940 to 1943. He graduated with first-class honors in English literature and subsequently joined the Canadian navy. After the war, he studied at the University of Toronto, and received a Ph.D. degree in 1950. In 1955/56 he was in Paris on a Canadian Government Overseas Fellowship in Creative Writing. He received the Governor-General's award for poetry, for **Friday's Child,** published in 1955. He also received a British Council prize for the best first book of verse published in England between 1953 and 1955. He is married to Sheila Watson nee Doherty, author of the novel **The Double Hook.** He is an associate professor of English at the University of Alberta. This year, in collaboration with Gordon Peacock, he has begun "Interface", an organization to promote the writing and production of drama of first intensity.

-:- -:- -:- -:- -:-

—**First meeting of the Western Canadian Educational Theatre Conference,** April 6, 7, 8 at Studio Theatre. Anyone interested in theatre is eligible to attend. Details at Box Office.

—**Drama for a Summer Night**

An outdoor summer theatre in Edmonton . . . Planning has begun for a repertory outdoor theatre on the campus, operating from the middle of June through July. Although the opening date was originally scheduled for June, 1963, it appears that it may now be possible to begin the project this summer . . . playing three nights a week in a revolving repertoire of drama for a summer night.

Cockcrow and the Gulls theatre program, back cover, announcing the inaugural Western Canadian Educational Theatre Conference hosted by Studio Theatre and plans for Torches summer theatre (95-639)

Several *Cockcrow*-related initiatives testify to Watson's quickening relation with Peacock and Studio Theatre. The first, TheatreScript, developed out of Peacock's decision that the Alumni Players would not only perform more experimental theatre on the contemporary French model but also produce new Canadian plays. Watson worked with Peacock on Theatrescript. His notebooks contain a draft announcement

Watson in the theatre, early 1960s; unidentified photographer (95-24-10)

declaring its aims: "to promote the production and writing of new Canadian drama of the highest possible calibre." TheatreScript offers its services to script editors, playwrights, "experienced writers who wanted to write for the stage," and to "young writers of proven talent." To the playwright, TheatreScript offers "every opportunity to have his new play read and to bring him into contact with theatre groups likely to produce his play" (91-36). In its first year of operation, TheatreScript — now Interface — ran from November 1961 through April 1962. Watson was listed as the secretary and presumably the primary contact at Studio Theatre.

If Interface were to prove successful in identifying and developing new Canadian plays, Edmonton would require additional venues in which those plays could be produced. Among the actors in *Cockcrow and the Gulls* was Bud D'Amur, who played Wrath. He had served on the executive of Walterdale Playhouse and in 1964 became manager of Yardbird Suite, a jazz club that had opened on Whyte Avenue in March 1957. From 1964 to its closing in August 1966, the Yardbird served as a showcase

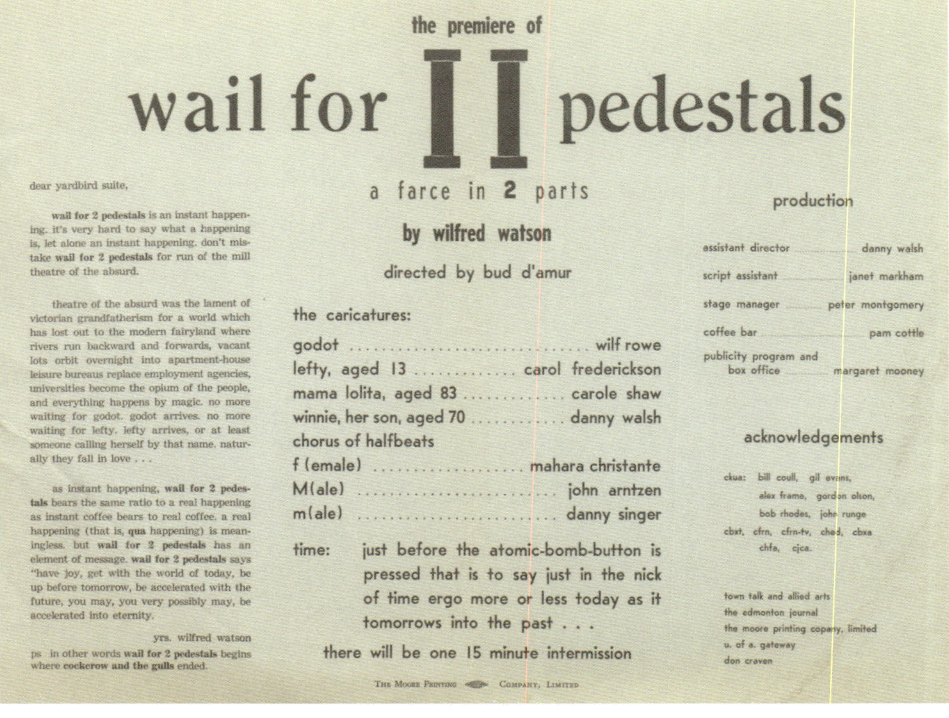

the premiere of

wail for II pedestals

dear yardbird suite,

wail for 2 pedestals is an instant happening. it's very hard to say what a happening is, let alone an instant happening. don't mistake **wail for 2 pedestals** for run of the mill theatre of the absurd.

theatre of the absurd was the lament of victorian grandfatherism for a world which has lost out to the modern fairyland where rivers run backward and forwards, vacant lots orbit overnight into apartment-house leisure bureaus replace employment agencies, universities become the opium of the people, and everything happens by magic. no more waiting for godot. godot arrives. no more waiting for lefty. lefty arrives, or at least someone calling herself by that name. naturally they fall in love . . .

as instant happening, **wail for 2 pedestals** bears the same ratio to a real happening as instant coffee bears to real coffee. a real happening (that is, **qua** happening) is meaningless. but **wail for 2 pedestals** has an element of message. **wail for 2 pedestals** says "have joy, get with the world of today, be up before tomorrow, be accelerated with the future, you may, you very possibly may, be accelerated into eternity.

yrs. wilfred watson

ps in other words **wail for 2 pedestals** begins where **cockcrow and the gulls** ended.

a farce in **2** parts

by wilfred watson

directed by bud d'amur

the caricatures:

godot .... wilf rowe
lefty, aged 13 .... carol frederickson
mama lolita, aged 83 .... carole shaw
winnie, her son, aged 70 .... danny walsh
chorus of halfbeats
f (emale) .... mahara christante
M(ale) .... john arntzen
m(ale) .... danny singer

time: just before the atomic-bomb-button is pressed that is to say just in the nick of time ergo more or less today as it tomorrows into the past . . .

there will be one 15 minute intermission

THE MOORE PRINTING COMPANY, LIMITED

production

assistant director .... danny walsh
script assistant .... janet markham
stage manager .... peter montgomery
coffee bar .... pam cottle
publicity program and box office .... margaret mooney

acknowledgements

ckua: bill coull, gil evans, alex frame, gordon olson, bob rhodes, john runge
cbxt, cfrn, cfrn-tv, ched, cbxa chfa, cjca.

town talk and allied arts
the edmonton journal
the moore printing copany, limited
u. of a. gateway
don craven

Wail for Two Pedestals theatre program (91-65)

for experimental theatre. The first Watson play produced at the Yardbird was *Wail for Two Pedestals: A Farce in Three Acts*; directed by Bud D'Amur, it opened on November 3, 1964 and ran for five nights. (It was subsequently performed in Calgary on January 15–16, 1965, and for the Western Educational Theatre Conference on April 5, 1965.) Other Watson plays produced at the Yardbird include "Chez-vous, Comfortable Pew" (May 1965) — which includes among its characters "Bud Demure," a "cultural Robin Hood" — "Tom Jones Meets Fanny Hill" (October 1965), and "Thing in Black" (March 1966).

In the program for *Cockcrow and the Gulls*, Studio Theatre announced yet another initiative, plans for Torches, an outdoor summer theatre. Each Torches season included an evening of readings titled *From Under the Black Bridge*. In the summer of 1962, the program, directed by Kathleen Stafford and Thomas Peacocke, included Watson, who read three poems from "The Ballad of Faustus," eight Jenny Blake "A Bawl of Wool" poems, and seven additional poems (91-65). In subsequent years, however, Watson was involved in organizing the event and developing a script that Peacocke would direct. (He did not include his own writing in these programs.) On at least two occasions, Studio Theatre adapted this format for use outside the Torches summer program: one commemorated President John F. Kennedy following his assassination; another marked the quatercentenary of Shakespeare's birth (91-65). Watson developed the script for both events. The typescript for the former opens with a passage from Marshall McLuhan's *The Gutenberg Galaxy*:

THE TORCHES THEATRE
in conjunction with Studio Theatre

presents

KAY MARTIN · **GARRY MITCHELL** · **ROBERT MUMFORD**
MAUREEN MURPHY · **THOMAS PEACOCKE**
HUTCH SHANDRO · **KATHLEEN STAFFORD** · **KENNETH WELSH**

in

From Under the Black Bridge

A READING

featuring the verse of

Mary Humphreys Baldridge · **Eli Mandel**
Robin Mathews · **Adeline Marcinow** · **Wilfred Watson**

Edited and Directed by Kathleen Stafford and Thomas Peacocke

THE PROGRAMME

Please withhold applause until end of sections.

PART ONE

"Epilogue to Hassan" .... James Elroy Flecker (1884-1915)

The Ways of Love

"A Passionate Shepherd to His Love" ... Christopher Marlowe (1564-1593)
"The Nymph's Reply" .... Sir Walter Raleigh (1552-1618)
"Song" .... C. Day Lewis (1904-)
"Song" .... Christina Georgina Rosetti (1830-1894)
"Why So Pale and Wan?" .... Sir John Suckling (1609-1642)
"Let the Toast Pass" .... Richard Brinsley Sheridan (1751-1816)

Some "Comments" on Marriage and Love by Oscar Wilde (1856-1900)

Of Men and Women

"The Rabbit Hunter" .... Robert Frost (1875-)
"Mrs. Hague" .... Osbert Sitwell (1892-)
"My Last Duchess" .... Robert Browning (1812-1889)
"The Looking Glass" .... Rudyard Kipling (1865-1936)
"Sally in Our Alley" .... Henry Carey (1693-1743)
"An Old Woman of the Roads" .... Padraic Colum (1881-)

INTERMISSION

PART TWO

FROM UNDER THE BLACK BRIDGE

Three Poems from a suite of poems "The Ballad of Faustus" .... **Wilfred Watson**
Part Two .... "Of all the lonely rivers"
Part Four .... "Polchuk is a janitor"
Part Five .... "Day after day adds up, she thought"

Familiar Places
"Snow White" .... Eli Mandel
"In Winter the Prairies" .... Robin Mathews
"Landscape Near Malton" .... Eli Mandel

From "A Bawl of Wool"—poems by Jenny Blake .... **Wilfred Watson**
Pome for a dead soldier
Pome of a church
Pome of windows
Pome of spring
Pome of hair
Pome of autumn
Pome of Helen of Troy
Pome of smells

A Miscellany
"A White Moon" .... Mary Humphreys Baldridge
"The Eye" .... Adeline Marcinow
"The Necklace" .... Wilfred Watson
"Rapunzel" .... Eli Mandel
"And You Too Raymond Souster" ... Eli Mandel
"Come Lover to Beauty" .... Robin Mathews
"Lines of Hubris" .... Wilfred Watson

Flora and Fauna
"Sermon on Bears" .... Wilfred Watson
"Blackbird" .... Mary Humphreys Baldridge
"The Hawk" .... Wilfred Watson
"Blackberry Pickers" .... Wilfred Watson
"Jellyfish" .... Robin Mathews
"Chrysanthemums" .... Wilfred Watson
"Man and Beast" .... Mary Humphreys Baldridge
"Arpeggio" .... Adeline Marcinow

"A Song for the End of Winter" .... **Wilfred Watson**

Poets at Play
"The Turtle" .... Ogden Nash (1902-)
"The Pig" .... Ogden Nash (1902-)
"A Shot at Random" .... D. B. W. Lewis (1894-)
"Infant Innocence" .... A. E. Housman (1859-1936)
"Cruel Clever Cat" .... Geoffrey Taylor
"A Christian" .... Thomas Russell Ybarra
"The Sorrows of Werther" .... William Makepeace Thackeray (1811-1863)
"The Painted Woman" .... Percy Bysshe Shelly (1792-1822)
"The Jumblies" .... Edward Lear (1812-1888)

Envoi
"How many miles to Babylon" .... Anon.
"Good morrow masters put your torches out" .... William Shakespeare (1564-1616)

Preliminary Announcement
The Fall Season at Studio Theatre
Juno and The Paycock .... **Oct. 18, 19, 20, 26, 27**
The Marionette Theatre of Peter Arnott ...... **Nov. 22, 23, 24**
J.B. .... **Feb. 21, 22, 23, Mar. 1, 2**

The Torches Theatre thanks you for your support and interest which has made the first season so successful.

Inaugural program, "From Under the Black Bridge," summer 1962, featuring Watson (91-65)

STUDIO THEATRE
UNIVERSITY OF ALBERTA

presents

THE ALUMNI PLAYERS

JEAN CLARKE STUART CARSON LOIS JHA
ELSIE PARK GOWAN GARRY MITCHELL VIVIEN MORDECAI
DAVID MURRAY HUTCH SHANDRO

in

THE BARD'S BIRTHDAY

directed by
THOMAS PEACOCKE

and featuring
a commemorative reading from Shakespeare's
writings arranged by Wilfred Watson

THE PROGRAMME

The Party Begins
Sonnet 55—Not Marble, nor the gilded monuments .... Garry Mitchell

Love is a Dog's Life
from TWO GENTLEMEN OF VERONA .... Stuart Carson

But the Party Grows Amorous
Sonnet 1—From fairest creatures we desire increase .... Elsie Park Gowan
Sonnet 2—When forth winters .... Jean Clarke
Sonnet 6—Then let not winter's ragged hand .... Stuart Carson
Sonnet 7—Lo, in the orient .... Elsie Park Gowan
Sonnet 10—For shame .... Hutch Shandro
Sonnet 12—When I do count the clock .... Lois Jha
Sonnet 16—But Wherefore do not you .... Vivien Mordecai
Sonnet 19—Devouring time .... Garry Mitchell
Sonnet 20—A Woman's face, with Nature's own hand painted .... David Murray

The Party Waxes Lyrical
Come away, come away, Death
I am gone, sir
The master, the swabber, the boatswain and I
Come unto these yellow sands
Full fathom five thy father lies

But the Path of True Love
from ROMEO AND JULIET .... Lois Jha, Garry Mitchell, Stuart Carson

Never Runs Smooth
Sonnet 94—They that have power to hurt .... David Murray

Because Venus
from VENUS AND ADONIS .... Vivien Mordecai and cast
Sonnet 64—Tired with all these for restful death I cry

Favours Machiavellian Hunchbacks
from RICHARD III .... Jean Clarke and David Murray

So Let We the Canakin Clink
Drinking song from OTHELLO

INTERMISSION

Part Two: The Party Unbends
In Case You Are In Any Doubt
Some early testimonials to the worth of Shakespeare:
John Milton—What needs my Shakespeare for his honoured bones .... Stuart Carson
Tributes from the First Folio .... Lois Jha, Garry Mitchell, Vivien Mordecai, Hutch Shandro and Stuart Carson

Enter the Dark Lady
Sonnet 130—My mistress' eyes are nothing like the sun .... Hutch Shandro
Sonnet 129—The expense of spirit .... Elsie Park Gowan
Sonnet 144—Two loves have I .... Hutch Shandro
Sonnet 146—Poor soul, the centre of my sinful earth .... Jean Clarke
Sonnet 138—When my love swears that she is made of Truth .... Hutch Shandro
from John Audrey's BRIEF LIVES .... Stuart Carson
Sonnet 141—In faith, I do not love thee with mine eyes .... Hutch Shandro
from THE TAMING OF THE SHREW .... Vivien Mordecai and Garry Mitchell

The Lion and the Fox
from Thomas Rymer's A SHORT VIEW OF TRAGEDY .... Elsie Park Gowan
from OTHELLO .... Jean Clarke, David Murray and Garry Mitchell
from OTHELLO—Desdemona's song .... Jean Clarke
from P. Wyndham Lewis's THE LION AND THE FOX .... Lois Jha and David Murray
from RICHARD II .... Hutch Shandro and Garry Mitchell
from THE MERRY WIVES OF WINDSOR .... Lois Jha and Stuart Carson

Time's Thievish Progress to Eternity
from AS YOU LIKE IT .... Hutch Shandro
from HAMLET .... Entire cast
from A MIDSUMMER NIGHT'S DREAM .... Garry Mitchell and David Murray
Twentieth-century (pop art) Shakespeare
from T. S. Eliot, CORIOLANUS, James Joyce, MACBETH, Samuel Beckett, MACBETH, George Barker, KING LEAR, William Butler Yeats, ANTHONY AND CLEOPATRA, Edward Albee

Epilogue
from TWELFTH NIGHT—When that I was a little tiny boy
Shakespeare's epitaph—Good friend, for Jesus' sake forbear .... Lois Jha

-:- -:- -:-

Coming—Drama For a Summer Night
Leave it to Jane alternating with **Picnic**
July 14 to Aug. 8—Tues. thru Sat.
at The Outdoor Torches Theatre

Left:
Program for "The Bard's Birthday," celebrating the 400th anniversary of Shakespeare's birth, April 26 1564 (91-65)

Below:
Program, "From Under the Black Bridge," commemorating John F. Kennedy (95-639)

the torches theatre presents:—

jean clarke mary glenfield susan mcfarlane stuart carson walter kaasa douglas riske thomas peacocke phil shragge on drums in

FROM UNDER THE BLACK BRIDGE

featuring a memorial reading for John Fitzgerald Kennedy on a theme suggested by H. M. McLuhan, the gutenberg galaxy, p. 278:

"Consistently, the twentieth century . . . this dramatic struggle of unlike modes of human insight and outlook has resulted in the greatest of all human ages, whether in the arts or in the sciences . . . . The new electric galaxy of events has already moved deeply into the Gutenberg galaxy. Even without collision, such existence of technologies and awareness brings trauma and tension to every living person. Our most ordinary and conventional attitudes seem suddenly twisted into gargoyles and grotesques. Familiar institutions and associations seem at times menacing and malignant."

script by wilfred watson **thomas peacocke directs it.**

programme part one:—

allen	FOOTNOTE TO HOWL	ginsberg
lawrence	I AM WAITING	ferlinghetti
anon	CAROL	medieval
miriam	MY LESSONS IN JAIL	waddington
margaret	APOCALYPTIC	avison
lawrence	JOHNNY NOLAN	ferlinghetti
lawrence	THE ARE PUTTING UP A STATUE	ferlinghetti
lawrence	I HAVE NOT LAIN WITH BEAUTY ALL MY LIFE	ferlinghetti
w.b.	LEDA AND THE SWAN	yeats
w.b.	HE AND SHE	yeats
w.b.	HIS BARGAIN	yeats
kathleen	LOVE POEM	raine
miriam	THE WOMAN'S JAIL	waddington
w.b.	POLITICS	yeats
w.b.	THE CURSE OF CROMWELL (interrupted)	yeats
andrew	HORATIAN ODE ON CROMWELL'S RETURN FROM IRELAND	marvell
w.b.	THE CURSE OF CROMWELL	yeats
lawrence	JUNKMAN'S OBLIGATO	ferlinghetti
helen	I LOVE MY LOVE	adam

intermission

programme part two:—

w.b.	THE SECOND COMING	yeats
ruth	LAMIA	calder
e.e.	MY FATHER MOVED THROUGH DOOMS OF LOVE	cummings
ronald	DEDALUS	oates
negro	GO DOWN, MOSES	spiritual
e.e.	POEM OR BEAUTY HURTS MR. VINAL	cummings
james	SMALL BABE TELL ME	reaney
james	SO YOU'VE LEARNED TO WALK	reaney
james	HELLO ERIC	reaney
walt	WHEN LILACS LAST IN THE DOORYARD BLOOM'D	whitman
walt	O! CAPTAIN! MY CAPTAIN (in memory of John Fitzgerald Kennedy)	whitman
jay	ORDINARY PEOPLE IN THE LAST DAYS	macpherson

end of programme.

sources for canadian verse selections:— miriam waddington, the season's lovers (ryerson, toronto, 1958) . . . margaret avison, winter sun and other poems (university of toronto press, 1960) . . . ruth calder, author's script . . . ronald bates, the wandering world (macmillan, toronto, 1959) .. . james reaney, the killdeer and other plays (macmillan, toronto, 1962) . . . jay macpherson, the boatman (oxford university press, toronto, 1957).

> . . . The new electric galaxy has already moved deeply into the Gutenberg galaxy. Even without collision, such co-existence of technologies and awareness brings trauma and tension to every living person. Our most ordinary and conventional attitudes seem suddenly twisted into gargoyles and grotesques. Familiar institutions seem . . . menacing and malignant. (95-50)

Television had brought Kennedy's assassination into living rooms everywhere, and Watson, who was engaged in a dialogue with McLuhan concerning the "new electric galaxy," saw the event, in part, through the lens of technological change.

Although Watson found his "small theatre group" at Edmonton's Studio Theatre, in the early 1960s his plays were also being produced elsewhere: in February 1962, shortly before Studio Theatre produced *Cockcrow and the Gulls*, Jack Sherriff directed a revision of "The Whatnot" for the Acadia University Drama Workshop; and in April 1963, Michael Tait directed the University of Toronto Alumni Players in Watson's new play, *The Trial of Corporal Adam*, at Coach House Theatre. The latter production won the *Toronto Telegram*'s annual theatre award for the best new play of the 1962–63 season. In that year, too, Watson's ongoing dialogue with Marshall McLuhan about the new electric galaxy was transformed into a collaborative book project titled *From Cliché to Archetype*.

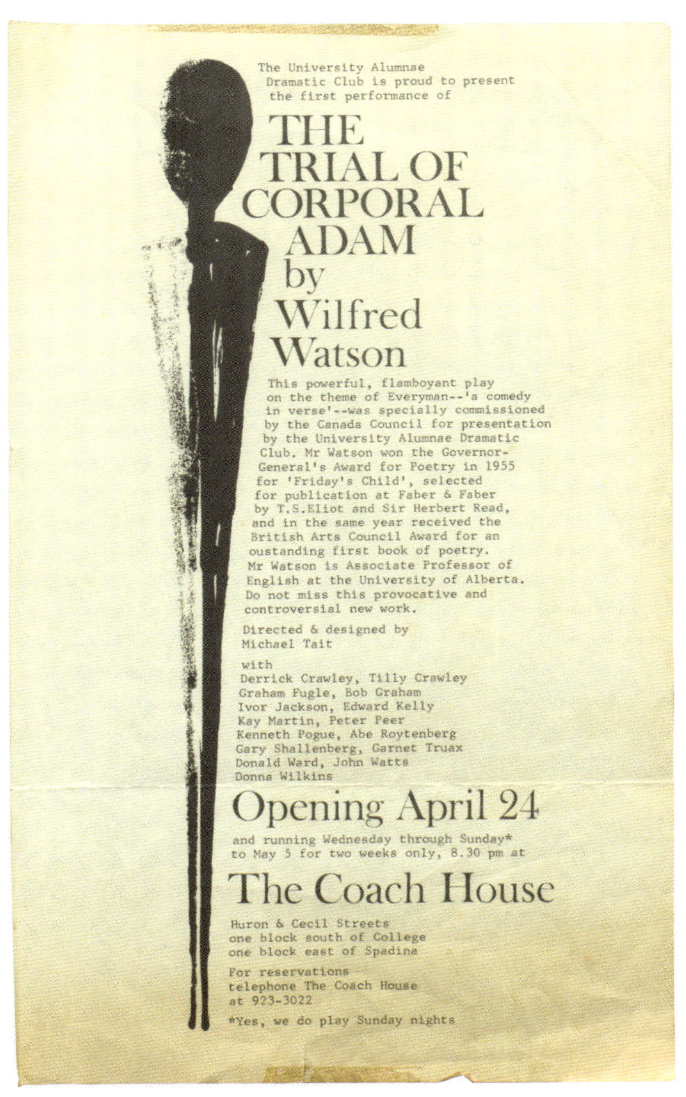

The University Alumnae Dramatic Club is proud to present the first performance of
THE TRIAL OF CORPORAL ADAM
by Wilfred Watson
This powerful, flamboyant play on the theme of Everyman--'a comedy in verse'--was specially commissioned by the Canada Council for presentation by the University Alumnae Dramatic Club. Mr Watson won the Governor-General's Award for Poetry in 1955 for 'Friday's Child', selected for publication at Faber & Faber by T.S.Eliot and Sir Herbert Read, and in the same year received the British Arts Council Award for an oustanding first book of poetry. Mr Watson is Associate Professor of English at the University of Alberta. Do not miss this provocative and controversial new work.
Directed & designed by Michael Tait
with
Derrick Crawley, Tilly Crawley
Graham Fugle, Bob Graham
Ivor Jackson, Edward Kelly
Kay Martin, Peter Peer
Kenneth Pogue, Abe Roytenberg
Gary Shallenberg, Garnet Truax
Donald Ward, John Watts
Donna Wilkins
Opening April 24
and running Wednesday through Sunday* to May 5 for two weeks only, 8.30 pm at
The Coach House
Huron & Cecil Streets
one block south of College
one block east of Spadina
For reservations telephone The Coach House at 923-3022
*Yes, we do play Sunday nights

Poster announcing *The Trial of Corporal Adam* (95-639)

Facing page:
Watson in undated Introduction to *From Cliché to Archetype*: "I first met him when I was a graduate student in Toronto. I think it was 1947" (95-99)

Collaborating with McLuhan

The University of Toronto hired McLuhan in 1946, one year after Wilfred Watson's arrival on campus; however, the two men appear to have met only once during Watson's years as a graduate student there, and that a chance meeting following a play, a production of Sidney Howard's *The Silver Cord*, at St. Michael's College (Flahiff 64; 95-99). Chance also seems to have governed Watson's introduction to McLuhan's writing: while in Toronto for the annual Humanities Association meeting in 1952, Watson chanced upon McLuhan's first book, *The Mechanical Bride: Folklore of Industrial Man*, purchased it, and wrote approvingly of it to Sheila Watson. It was through Sheila Watson — specifically, her interest in Modernist British author and painter Wyndham Lewis — that Wilfred Watson and McLuhan eventually met and became friends. When she entered the graduate program in English at the University of Toronto in 1956 and chose to focus her doctorate on Lewis, McLuhan became her supervisor (Flahiff 176). When they met, Watson remembered, McLuhan "invited, urged me, to join in his approach to literature — to see it as an exploration of the technological strains that were brought about by man's attempt to exteriorize his needs" (91-240 Apr 10 1980). The relationship

From Cliché to Archetype, introduction

From Cliche' to Archetype was projected sometime between 1962 snd 1963, at a time when Professor McLuhan was strenuously defending the two epoch-making studies, The Gutenberg Galaxy and Understanding Media. I have generally been his student, although I am slightly senior -- he was born in Edmonton, Alberta in July, 1911, and I was born in Rochester, England in May of the same year. I was drawn to him because I felt he had something to teach me about the writing of drama, which is and has been a passionate pre-occupation of mine. He was at this time teaching at the University of Toronto, and I was teaching at the University of Alberta. I first met him when I was a graduate student at Toronto. I think it was in 1947. I had gone to my first experience of theatre in the round, a performance at St. Michael's College of Sidney Howard's play about mother love: The Silver Chord. There was no formal introduction. Marshall walked back with me, after the performance, across the campus, and I should have been exasperated, I suppose, if the performance hadn't been so devastatingly enervating, by his explanations of the effects of Sidney Howard's play. The tiny audience sat a few inches away from the actors, and the result was that of a series of ghastly family rows. Marshall cheerfully surmised that the effect would have been even greater if the actors had been professional. Our respective homes were both on the other side of Bloor Street, so we argued the the pros and cons of amateur vs professional performance for the length of Philosopher's Walk, a long path which connects Queen's Park with Bloor street, and which separated the Museum of Fine Arts from the University of Toronto Stadium, the Conservatory of Music and a old

between Watson and McLuhan developed slowly, however, because the two men lived a considerable distance from one another, because Watson was in the midst of developing his relationship with Peacock and Studio Theatre, and also, perhaps, because McLuhan was Sheila Watson's supervisor. It was not until 1963 that Watson and McLuhan decided to write *From Cliché to Archetype* together; it was not until 1965 that they jointly entered into a contract with Viking Press.

Timing is important. When they decided to collaborate on the book, both men were entering their most productive decades as writers: McLuhan had published *Gutenberg Galaxy: The Making of Typographic Man* (1962) and was just completing *Understanding Media: The Extensions of Man* (1964); Watson had not only authored the award-winning *Friday's Child* but, with successful productions of "The Whatnot," *Cockcrow and the Gulls,* and *The Trial of Corporal Adam* to his credit, had also established himself as an avant-garde playwright. The intellectual exchange between them is truly remarkable and well documented in Watson's extant papers: in the many letters they exchanged, in Watson's notebooks and journals, and in his drafts of the text they were co-authoring. The papers enable study not only of the genesis of *From Cliché to Archetype*, but also of Watson's engagement with McLuhan's media theory and his probing of that theory in his poetry and plays.

Watson and McLuhan had much in common. As scholars, they shared a strong interest both in the early modern period — that is, in the centuries that gave rise to print culture — and in Modernism, the movement that heralded its decline. Both men shared an interest in language, particularly in how it had been transformed by the advent of print and was continuing to change with the introduction of new media. Both men were autodidacts as well as traditionally educated scholars, whose wide-ranging interests prompted them to seek intellectual community across disciplinary boundaries and beyond the academy. Where Watson found his intellectual home in Studio Theatre, McLuhan sought his in the Centre for Culture and Technology created for him by the University of Toronto in 1963. Both felt increasingly marginalized within their own disciplines and universities. In a period of growing cultural nationalism in Canada, McLuhan, like Watson, preferred to think beyond the nation. Although by the late 1960s McLuhan's reputation had eclipsed Watson's, in the early '60s both were Governor General's Award winners, McLuhan having won his for *Gutenberg Galaxy*.

In 1959, however, the two men were relatively new acquaintances. Watson spent the summer of 1959 in Toronto and the first exchange of letters between them dates from that fall. On September 8, 1959, Watson sends McLuhan news clippings from the *Edmonton Journal* and the *CBC Times* and writes, "I find your ideas extremely stimulating — I think you are the only person at Toronto I ever got an idea from" (Flahiff 245). Despite Watson's initial enthusiasm, in their first four years of friendship, that is, between 1959 and 1963, they exchanged only a handful of letters. They may not have met again until 1961. In June of that year Watson and McLuhan were in the audience for papers each presented at the Humanities Association of Canada annual meeting in Montreal: Watson's on "Instructuralization in Drama and the Other Arts," McLuhan's on "The Humanities in the Electric Age." Reflecting on the genesis of *From Cliché to Archetype* years later in a letter to William Toye, Watson terms the Montreal

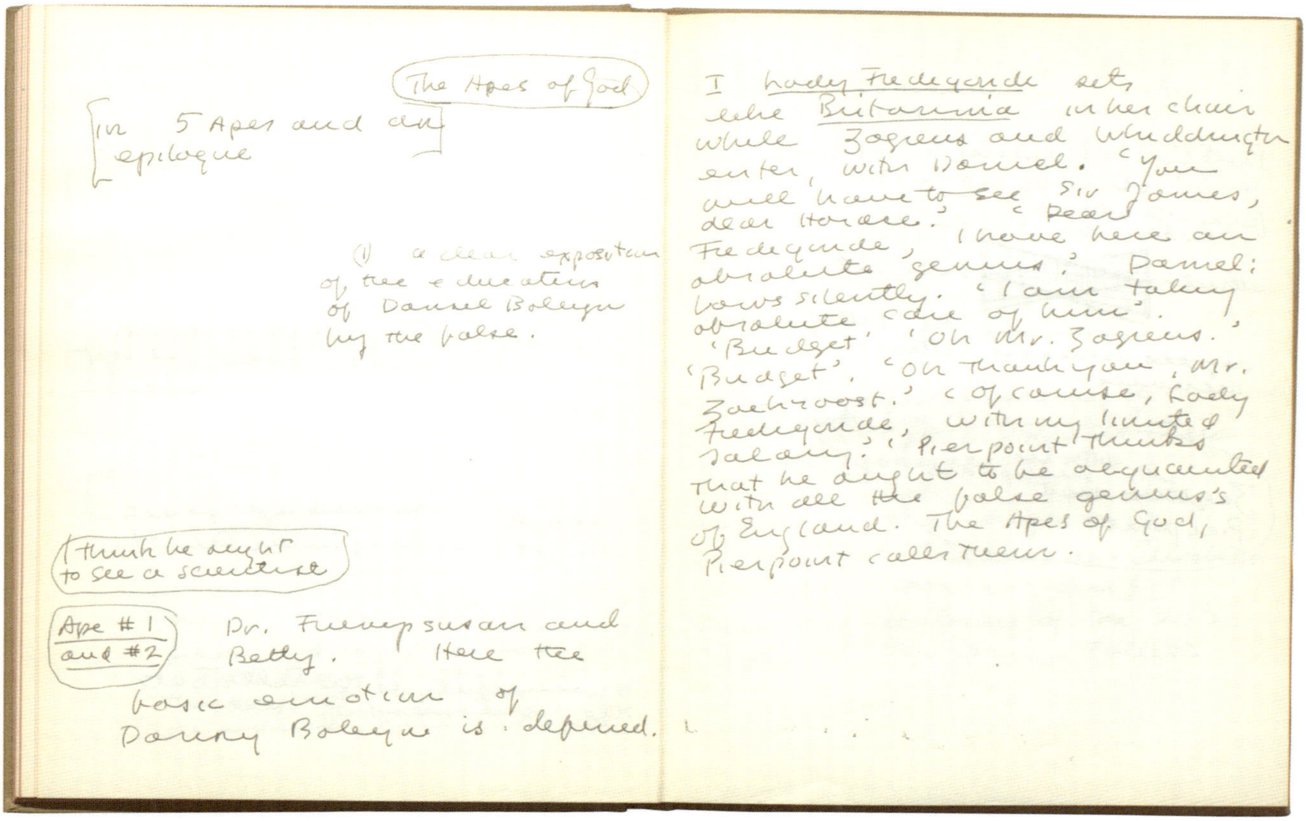

Scenario for an adaptation of *The Apes of God*; journal entry Oct 1961 (91-66)

papers "a sort of blueprint" for their subsequent book (95-132 Feb 5 1987). Although the meeting in Montreal was followed a week later by another in Toronto — where Watson again spent the summer — there is no evidence in the notebooks and journals for 1961 either that he is thinking through cliché and archetype-related issues or that he and McLuhan are collaborating. That work would not begin for another two years and more, that is, after the production of *Cockcrow* in Edmonton and of *Corporal Adam* in Toronto and after the publication of *Gutenberg Galaxy*.

There were, however, other, related projects. If, in the early years, the relationship between the two men was mediated by Sheila Watson, that mediation took at least two forms: the first, direct; the second, indirect. The direct form was her suggestion to Wilfred in 1959 that he consider adapting McLuhan's *The Mechanical Bride* for stage. Although he initially embraced the idea and in a letter to McLuhan on June 29, 1961 reports having completed forty pages of a script, he subsequently abandoned the project. The indirect form of mediation was Sheila Watson's doctoral study itself. Her engagement with Wyndham Lewis's *oeuvre* prompted Wilfred, between the mid-1950s and the mid-1960s, to read (or re-read) most of Lewis's books. In August 1961, while in Toronto for the summer, he re-read Lewis's novel *The Apes of God* and began imagining how he might adapt it for stage (91-64). At the same time, he read and made notes on McLuhan's doctoral study of the sixteenth-century dramatist, satirist, and pamphleteer Thomas Nashe and on an advance copy of *Gutenberg Galaxy* (91-66). Although he shelved the *Apes* project in the fall of that year, Watson returned to it in August 1963.

In a letter to Wilfred and Sheila Watson dated August 11, 1963, McLuhan, who had just returned from London (where, among other things, he met with Mrs. Lewis), congratulated Wilfred on the completion of *Another Bloody Page from Plutarch* and added: "Would be grand if you could drop in for a few days. Wilfred, you and I must knock off the Cliché to Archetype sometime before school begins" (MM 40-27).[28] This is McLuhan's first mention in these letters of the book project. Watson's occurs weeks later, in the same letter in which he announces the *Apes* project. "I should have answered [your letter]," he writes on September 3, "but I have been engrossed in a dramatization of *The Apes of God*, which is now some fifty pages (of a probable 75 or 80) pp. gone — an hour of playing time completed. I am enjoying myself immensely." He then adds: "I found I was completely swallowed up by the cliché/archetype book when I started work on it in May. I seemed to be probing into mysteries so deep that I wondered if the book mightn't demand a total sacrifice, if I went further"(MM 40-27). Watson had stayed with the McLuhans for a week in April when he was in Toronto to attend the premiere of *The Trial of Corporal Adam*. Presumably it was during this visit that the two men agreed to collaborate on the cliché/archetype book.[29] Although Watson completed his dramatization of *The Apes of God* in September 1963 and returned to it from time to time, it was never staged.

The two men struggled for five years to develop their book. In working together, they faced several problems. The first was simply that they lived at opposite ends of the country. Although they wrote one another frequently, spoke on the phone, and met in person when they could, collaborating at a distance proved a challenge. In January 1964, for example, McLuhan stopped over in Edmonton to meet with Watson. While such meetings proved energizing, they did not often translate into pages written. The second problem relates to the first: both men were arguably at the height of their careers and exceptionally busy, especially McLuhan, who, with the publication of *Understanding Media* in the spring of 1964, quickly became "Canada's intellectual comet" (Marchand 171). The fundamental problem, however, is that Watson and McLuhan struggled unsuccessfully to develop collaborative practices that would enable their work together. Thus, on July 7, 1964, after exchanging letters and ideas for a year, Watson writes: "I want some direction about how you think we cd. do the cliché/arch book. My own idea is that I shd. do write up I and you should take my draft and modify it by addition

& subtraction into write up II and then I could get this put into a final typescript" (Flahiff 245). Although McLuhan readily agreed with Watson's proposal — "Yep. You do the first draft. I'll do no. II . . . ." (Flahiff 245; 95-106 July 10 1964) — and their work entered a new stage, they had not addressed underlying problems in their collaboration.

Days after agreeing that Watson should write the first draft of C/A,[30] McLuhan declared: "We must do this together. A team is better than any solo effort if only because it permits dialogue and development and also manifests those qualities to the public" (Flahiff 244; 95-106 July 1964). They seem, however, to have had fundamentally different aims. McLuhan was intent on drawing out the implications of the two groundbreaking books he had already published, a goal that would lead to the posthumous appearance of *Laws of Media* (1988). Watson, on the other hand, was intent on probing McLuhan's perceptions — and his own — to test their worth. For McLuhan, the necessary knowledge was already in hand; for Watson, what was in hand needed probing. One index of the differing methods and goals was McLuhan's belief, reiterated frequently, that they could complete the book in a week of hard work in Toronto with his secretary, Margaret Stewart, versus Watson's desire that McLuhan rethink basic assumptions. Watson's conception of collaboration was arguably formed by his work in theatre: rehearsals were yet another stage of writing, challenging him to rethink basic assumptions and rewrite. As the composition of *From Cliché to Archetype* progressed, Watson came increasingly to feel that McLuhan wanted disciples, not collaborators.

Facing page:
"A note on radical absurdity" (95-110)

"Montaigne Never Read *Understanding Media*"

Judging from Watson's extant papers, the two men developed *From Cliché to Archetype* in at least five stages. In the first stage, from summer 1963 to summer 1964, they began the exchange of letters and ideas that would continue throughout their collaboration, probing their understanding of cliché and archetype and proposing directions in which to develop the book. Convinced he had much to learn as a dramatist from his collaborator, in stage one Watson began to explore the relevance of McLuhan's thinking to theatre. On February 11, 1964, shortly after McLuhan's visit to Edmonton, he wrote his co-author that he had completed several pages on theatre and *Gutenberg Galaxy* and that the results were "amazing." The publication of *Understanding Media* months later prompted Watson to rethink McLuhan's relevance to theatre yet again; this analysis led both to the poem "I shot a trumpet into my brain" and to the accompanying preface, "On Radical Absurdity," which opens with the statement "Montaigne never read *Understanding Media*. . . ."

A note on radical absurdity

Montaigne never read Understanding Media, yet there's a good deal of point to what he says about the relation between our animal and our human extensions:

> no use our mounting on stilts, for on stilts we must still walk on our own legs....on the loftiest throne in the world we still are sitting only on our own rump.

~~There is little reason to doubt but that he found himself~~ [That he discovered his métier] in the printed book, [sans doute] despite his ~~insisting upon the importance of~~ [protesting his attachment to] animal extensions like legs and rump. The [important] question ~~still~~ remains, where in the range of extensions do we locate our being? We have only to think of trumpeter and trumpet, instead of king and throne, to see ~~we are up against no easy problem.~~ [the problem.] Montaigne often chafes against ~~the restrictions of~~ the unified consciousness imposed by ~~the~~ print~~ed book~~, and a trumpeter, if his only mode of awareness was his trumpet, might likewise complain of limitation. Our worry is about freedom. Twentieth-century man has many modes of consciousness and with these goes a freedom not enjoyed by any previous civilization. It is this freedom, a very terrible freedom, a freedom radically unlike any other mankind has yet known, that I find myself wanting to celebrate in absurdist plays and in satirical verse. Satire is often a ritual of acceptance by means of which a Swift, a Sterne, or a Percy Wyndham Lewis castigates the crossing of lines, while recognizing the right of the future to innovate. Or it is exploration -- I won't claim that in my attempts at theatre of the absurd I have been engaged in exploration; celebrate is the right word. This new freedom I have been celebrating is really a very wonderful development-- it dictates the very unrealistic

The collaboration entered its second stage in July 1964 when Watson proposed that he assume responsibility for writing a first draft of C/A. In this stage, which extended from July 1964 to August 1965, they continued to exchange letters and ideas on the understanding that Watson would gather these ideas into the manuscript he was developing. When McLuhan agreed to Watson's proposal, the latter began work almost immediately. On July 16 he sent McLuhan an essay, "Australopithecus and the Electronic Brain," he had just drafted — examining McLuhan's ideas through the lens of Robert Ardrey's *African Genesis: A Personal Investigation Into Animal Origins and the Nature of Man* — and added: "Today I did a three page introduction to the Cliché/Archetype. I tacked it, the book, on to Galaxy & C and Media. — I will keep it until I finish a chapter, then send you . . . " (MM 40-27). Although Watson worked on the C/A book through the summer and early fall, he was not happy with the results. In the postscript to an October 14 letter, he wrote McLuhan:

> Wd like to spend the winter with you writing the Arch/Cliché study. You will say, you had the opp. this summer, but I wasn't ready. I got 30 odd pp. done. I am ready now. They are good pp. But I think I need to start afresh, since these were heuristic & tentative. (MM 40-27)

By the following May, however, when Viking Press offered a publishing contract — with a five-thousand-dollar advance — conditional on receipt of an outline and a chapter or two, Watson had the material more or less in hand (95-106 June 1965). On June 16 he sent McLuhan the outline and chapter one; McLuhan read them in mid-July and forwarded the chapter to Clay Felker at Viking on July 31 with a long cover letter, framing Watson's chapter within his own argument concerning the relation of old (archetype) and new (cliché) technologies (MM 40-27 August 15 1965).

That Watson's work in this second stage of composition was "heuristic and tentative" should not surprise, for the decision to collaborate was also a commitment to reread and rethink his co-author's work. That task was made more difficult by the fact that McLuhan was, at the time, in the process of articulating some of his key concepts: *Understanding Media* appeared only late in stage one. Watson not only read McLuhan's writing and conversed with him, but also tested McLuhan's ideas in various genres and venues: in the play, *Wail for Two Pedestals*, he began writing for Yardbird Suite; in the scripts he developed for *From Under the Black Bridge*; and in his poetry. Although developed for different occasions and audiences, these separate projects are also inextricably related, as Watson's projects almost invariably are. Thus, in a letter to McLuhan dated December 11, 1964, Watson attributes the success of *Wail* to his recognition of the two "emotional polarities" possible in the age of new media, "nostalgia and wonder":

Facing page:
"I set Godot up on one pedestal and Lefty . . . up on the other pedestal"; Watson to McLuhan Dec 11 1964 (95-106)

8918 Windsor Rd. Edmonton, Alta. Dec.11, 1964

Dear Marshall,

Thank you for various communications. Also for publishing Australopithecus and the e.b. It arrived on my desk just after first performance of a new play a post-Beatnik farce about Godot and Lefty. Local punditry much dismayed by my rejection of the theatre of the absurd, which begins to be understood à la Esslin who is so much out of touch as to believe that modern language is in a decline surely not never was English more fertile than now? But Wail for II pedestals was huge success in a grain of sand. Anyone whose sensibility had not advanced beyond that of an Albertan freshman (i.e. had not been Gutenburged) went wild about it.

I like your idea about art as the consciousness, technology as the unconsciousness, of the age.

Part of success of Wail for Two Peds resided in fact thzt I'd recognized two emotional polarities possible in this age, nostalgia and wonder. Progress alienates and creates nostalgia and hence the proliferation of scads of nostalgia pieces -- The Waste Land, etc. much of Joyce, as well as the continents of inverted nostalgia in Lewis. But Progress allso generates an equal sense of wonder, which I take to be the emotion appropriate to the marvelous. In practice, the genuine wonder is actually tinged with nostalgia-- it is wonder at the horror of....?

You will see that by contrasting these two basic emotions, I could get an almost brandnew sense of the modernity of the times in the theatre. I set Godot up on one pedestal and Lefty (I took the liberty of changing the sex of Odets' communist) up on the other pedestal, and let them fall in love to the tune of Camusian lamentation for the hopeless transcendence of the age.

Other technical advances in Wail I hope to exploit. Chiefly the use of chorus. Much help from Understanding Media -- I introduced acknowledgement in the climax of wail-- at rehearsal I feared this might be a fatuity, but such is your renown in these parts that it seemed beautifully right and at one performance the audience responded with a peal of laughter --but what I sought was the medium-metaphor. Grasped at the chorus-theme as the consicence of mankind, and then went on to use other parts of theatre metaphor-- including stage directions.

This chorus is wailing for you. Blessings,

Wilfred

P.S. Peter Montgomery you'll see was stage manager and a devoted one.

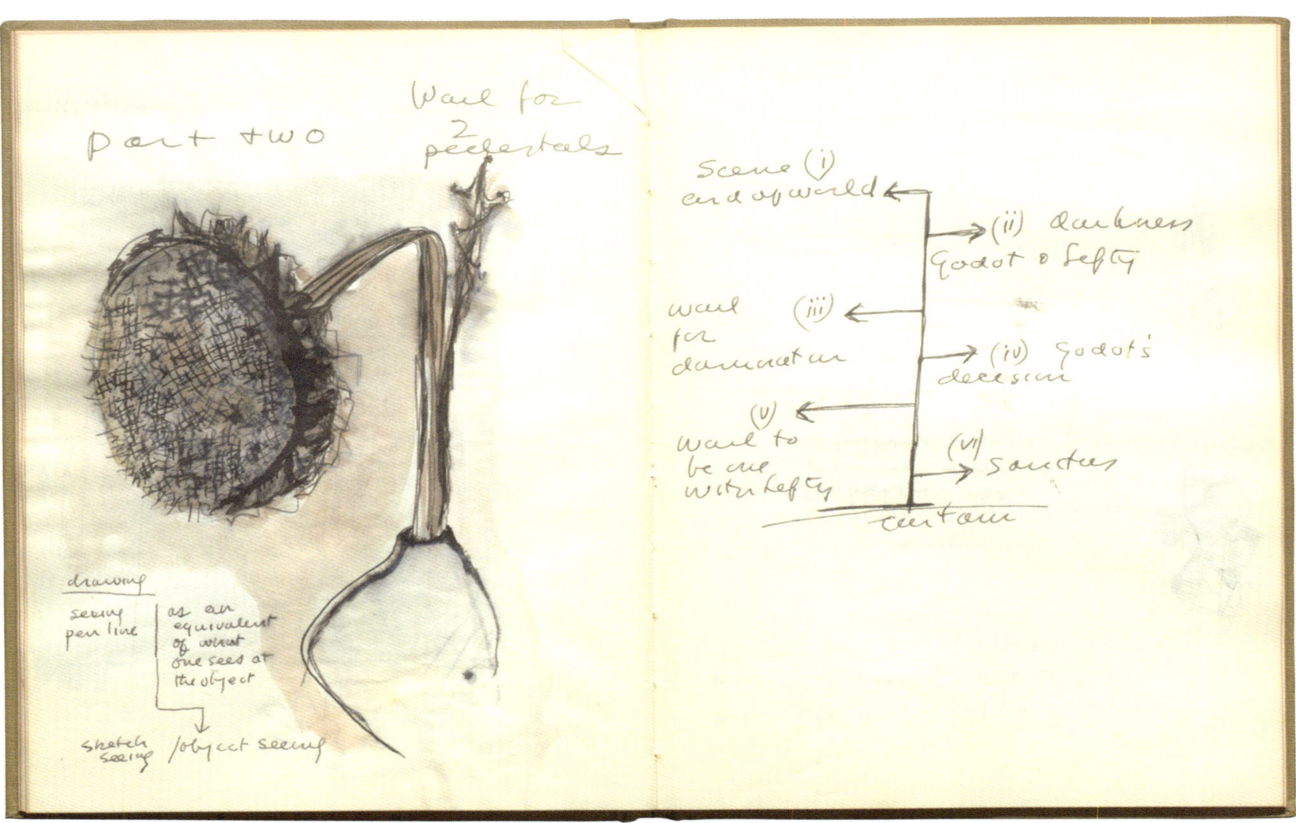

Outline for *Wail for Two Pedestals*; notebook entry, Aug–Sept 14 1964 (91-101)

> You will see that by contrasting these two basic emotions, I could get an almost brand new sense of the modernity of the times in the theatre. I set Godot up on one pedestal and Lefty (I took the liberty of changing the sex of Odets' communist) up on the other pedestal, and let them fall in love to the tune of Camusian lamentation for the hopeless transcendence of the age.
>
> Other technical advances in Wail I hope to exploit, chiefly the use of chorus. Much help from Understanding Media. I introduced acknowledgement in the climax of wail — . . . such is your renown in these parts that it seemed beautifully right and at one performance the audience responded with a peal of laughter — but what I sought was the medium metaphor. Grasped at the chorus-theme as the conscience of mankind, and then went on to use other parts of theatre metaphor — including stage directions. (95-06)

At every stage in his collaboration with McLuhan, one needs to examine Watson's work for their book in relation to his other writing.

Stage three in the composition of *From Cliché to Archetype* extends from the summer of 1965 through December 1966. When Watson and McLuhan signed with Viking, they felt a new sense of urgency about completing the book. McLuhan renewed his appeals that Watson join him in Toronto so they might work with Mrs. Stewart to finish the book, but settled, in the short term, for an early August stopover in Edmonton as part of a scheduled trip to San Francisco (organized by two California businessmen and "genius scouts" [Marchand 122–24]). Although McLuhan stated on more than one occasion that he was finally ready to write the C/A book, or that he was making good progress, other commitments and book projects intervened. By December 1965 he was dictating short chapters and sections, presumably to Mrs. Stewart, in an attempt to speed up the work, though he himself questioned whether this approach would prove satisfactory (95-106 Dec 29 1965).

There are at least two significant developments in stage three. The first is that Watson began to articulate the understanding of new media and multi-consciousness that would inform "McLuhan and Multi-consciousness: The Place Marie Dialogues," the essay in which he explains the breakdown in their collaboration. In a letter to McLuhan on June 15, 1966, he asked: "Would it be wrong to call media extensions of human consciousness? The 'medium is the message' then could be written the 'environment is the extension of consciousness.'"

"In the electronic age we have made possible many different kinds of consciousness?"; Watson to McLuhan June 15 1966 (95-107)

8910 Windsor Road,
Edmonton, Alta.

June 15, 1966

Dear Marshall,

Somewhere or other in Gutenberg Galaxy or more likely in U/Media there is some reference to "extension of consciousness"? I wonder if this idea doesn't need adaptation to our Cliche/Arch treatment of media? The extensions of man are developments of awarenss along certain material lines. Thus all media are extensions of consciousness as far as the material basis permits? Would it be wrong to call media extensions of consciousness? The "medium is the message" then could be written the "envronment is the extension of consciousness". Tied in with this equation is the problem of content. This is a medium within a medium, a consciousness within a consciousness?

What I am driving at, is the relation between the "me myself" and my awareness. I don't know exactly what are the right terms to use here. MAN = ONE OF MANKIND + ANIMAL EXTENSIONS + HUMAN EXTENSIONS. He is a mixture of awarenesses.

The notion that the conscious self is at the centre of man, is something that arises from the centrality of the speech-complex of media, oral, scriptural, print.

In the electronic age we have made possible many kinds of consciousness? The contemporary sense of alienation arises not from lack of identity between the ego or self and the chosen or adopted modes of consciousness but from the fact that there is no single dominant gradient if you like medium such as printing to supply a common consciousness to other egos or selves.

Unless my arguments here are wrong, this notion of the ego outfitting itself with public modes of consciousness could be very useful in the conclusion of the book?

Yours,

> The notion that the conscious self is at the centre of man, is something that arises from the centrality of the speech-complex of media, oral, scriptural, print.
>
> In the electronic age we have made possible many different kinds of consciousness? The contemporary sense of alienation arises not from a lack of identity between the ego or self and the chosen or adopted modes of consciousness but from the fact that there is no single dominant gradient if you like medium such as printing to supply a common consciousness to other egos or selves.
>
> Unless my arguments here are wrong, this notion of the ego outfitting itself with a public mode of consciousness could be very useful in the conclusion of the book? (95-107)

As Watson explained in a letter to McLuhan on July 2, he began articulating this position when he submitted "I shot a trumpet into my brain" for publication in *Canadian Literature* and George Woodcock asked "for an introduction on my views of theatre of the absurd, satire etc. as preamble to justify his publishing" the poem (MM 40-27).

The second development is McLuhan's acknowledgement, in a letter dated July 1, that there might be room for disagreement provided they agreed on the "general process" in the movement between cliché and archetype: "This would suggest that we put the whole book in the conditional and subjunctive, then we don't have to match ideas?" (95-107). In response, Watson sends McLuhan the "Note on radical absurdity" he developed for Woodcock and remarks in a postscript: "I don't worry too much about difference of opinion. When everything is put together, anything confusing can be blue-pencilled out?" (MM 40-27).

The two continued to struggle, however, to put everything together. In the fall of 1966, McLuhan was preoccupied with other work; in addition to numerous speaking engagements, he was "frantically attempting" (95-107 Nov 24 1966) to complete *Culture Is Our Business*, one of nine books he would publish between 1967 and 1970 (in addition to *From Cliché to Archetype*). He sought Watson's "tactical suggestions" about how best to respond to Viking's queries about the C/A manuscript (95-107 Sept 29 1966). Although Watson continued to work on the project, the flow of letters and ideas slowed.

The fourth stage of work on *From Cliché to Archetype*, from January 1967 to spring 1968, is the least clearly defined and thus, perhaps, most debatable. Salient developments in this stage include mounting pressure from Viking for a manuscript and the co-authors' increased willingness to consider alternative strategies to produce it. Watson was the first to propose an alternative strategy. The magazine *Saturday Night*, in its February 1967 issue, published three articles on love, including one by McLuhan in

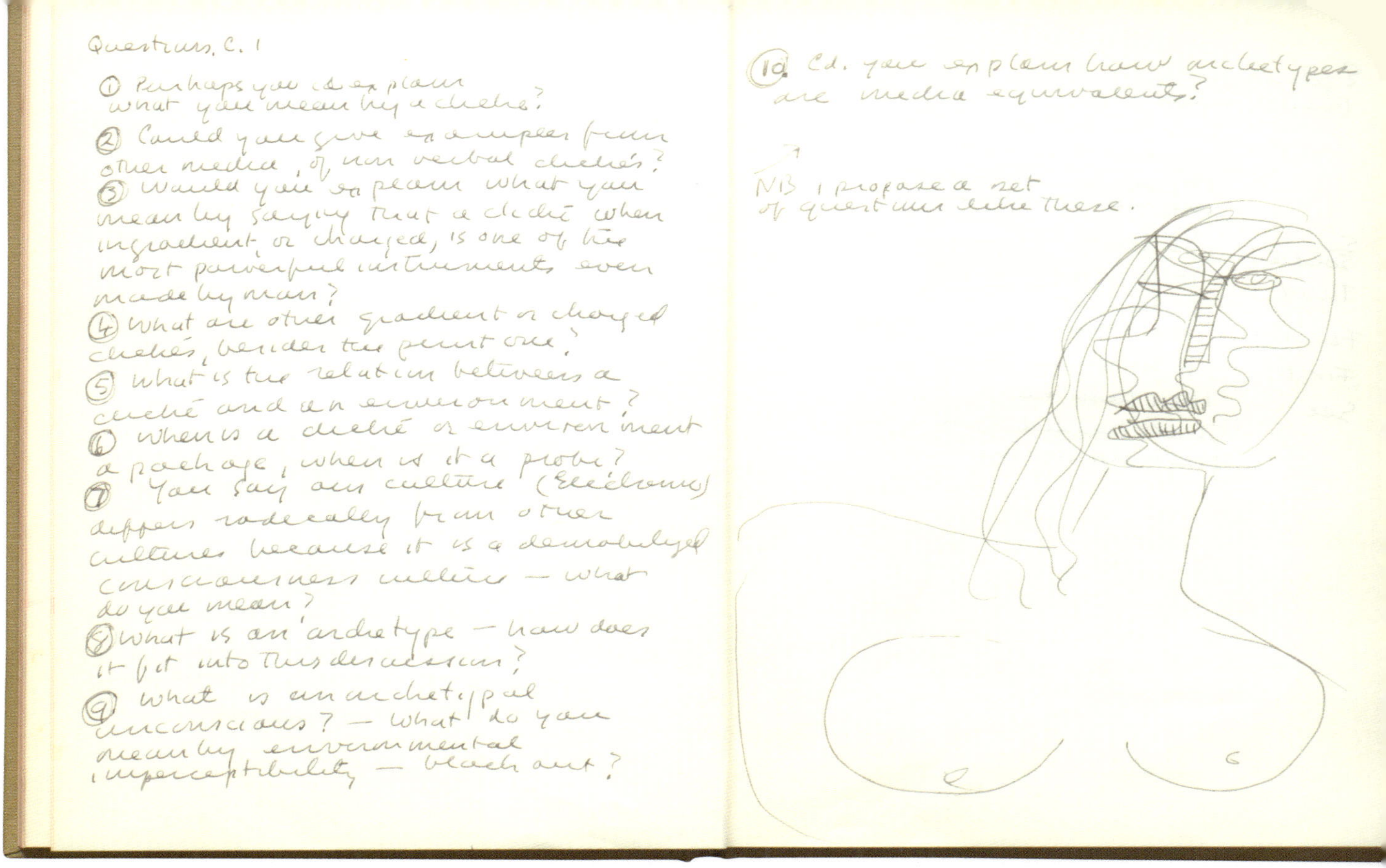

"Perhaps you could explain what you mean by cliché?"; Watson drafts questions for interview with McLuhan; journal entry Feb 4 1967 (91-137)

the form of an interview. After reading the article "with great hoots of delight" and developing various lines of argument in his notebook (91-137), Watson proposed to McLuhan that they use "the interview-form" for the C/A book:

> Suppose I prepared a whole series of questions to ask you, and then we put your answers on tape, and then transcribed them?
>
> Wouldn't this get the writing done quickly? And at the same time permit a cross-fertilization from me to you?
>
> Typographically, couldn't my questions occur at the heads of chapters, like the chapter headings of the *Gutenberg Galaxy*, which were so effective?
>
> If this idea appeals to you at all, I'd be quite eager to appear in Toronto sometime about the second week in May with a tape-recorder, some tapes, and a flock of prepared questions. Or at some other time in the summer. (MM 40-27 Feb 6 1967)

When he wrote McLuhan, Watson had already developed a first draft of possible questions, from "Perhaps you could explain what you mean by a cliché?" to "What is the relation between a cliché and an environment?" and "What is an archetype — how does it fit into this discussion?" (91-137 Feb 4 1967). Although McLuhan readily agreed to Watson's proposal (95-107 Feb 9 1967), there was no follow-up.

Why did Watson not act on this proposal? A partial explanation appears in a letter Watson writes McLuhan three weeks later:

> It was good to have direct word of you via Sheila, even though she felt that you were desperately in need of relief from the pressures that are being placed upon you. I hesitate to add to the strain, and will wait until you feel ready to do the C/A book, or start in earnest solus, or do it by the tape recorder or some oral technique. (95-107 Feb 26 1967)

By early 1967 members of McLuhan's inner circle and his family were increasingly concerned about his health; and yet, "unofficially, 1967 was the Year of McLuhan" and therefore no time to be ill (Gordon 226). Watson, who had two plays — "Thing in Black" and "The Canadian Fact" — in production over the winter, planned to resume work on *From Cliché to Archetype* at the end of term. Early in the new year, however, Centennial funding was put in place for a new play, to be produced by Studio Theatre and directed by Thomas Peacocke, and Watson spent the summer months writing and revising *O Holy Ghost, DIP YOUR FINGER IN THE BLOOD OF CANADA and write, I LOVE YOU.*

One of the many pressures on McLuhan was his decision to serve as the inaugural Albert Schweitzer Chair in Humanities at Fordham University in New York for 1967–68. He wanted to complete *From Cliché to Archetype* before he took up the appointment. When that plan failed, he arranged for the Watsons to join him in New York once *O Holy Ghost* (shortened to *DIP* by both cast and Watson) completed its run on December 9, 1967, with Viking Press advancing one thousand dollars to pay Wilfred's expenses (95-107 Oct 24 1967). (He remained confident the two men could finalize the manuscript quickly, that is, before Christmas.) On November 25, however, he underwent surgery to remove a brain tumor and plans to complete the C/A book in New York in December were abandoned. Early in 1968, a new plan emerged: McLuhan proposed to secure appointments for Wilfred and Sheila Watson as research associates in his Centre for Culture and Technology for the 1968–69 academic year, allowing the two men to complete *From Cliché to Archetype* with Mrs. Stewart, as McLuhan had always envisioned they would. What is more, there would be time aplenty to develop new projects. With this plan in place, stage four ends.

The final stage in the genesis of *From Cliché to Archetype*, which extends from spring 1968 to publication in fall 1970, has been the primary focus of published accounts of the Watson–McLuhan collaboration. When Watson joined the Centre for Culture and Technology as a Research Associate for 1968–69, and the two men finally sat down with Mrs. Stewart to complete their book, they had not only five years of notes each had accumulated on the subject but also the detailed chapter outlines Watson had developed with McLuhan's help and the various manuscripts Watson had taken the lead in developing. Watson also had had five years of experience testing McLuhan's theories on stage, most recently in the Studio Theatre's production of *DIP*.

McLuhan presumably also had access to a more recent version of *From Cliché to Archetype* Watson had developed: each page of this text is divided into four numbered quadrants, for a total of 444 quadrants in the extant 111-page typescript. Here, for example, are quadrants 345–348 on p. 87:

345 Poetry today flourishes as never before.	346 The theater from Ibsen to Eliot (the title of a remarkable survey of realistic theatre by Raymond Williams) has tried to censor out the new creative language which is based on the verbal surround of other technologies.
347 From Ibsen to Eliot, however, the theatre has become progressively less relevant and language has become incredibly more creative.	348 When at its best, contemporary language has taken its cue from the verbal surround which accompanies all human acts. (95-95)

The quadrant design calls into question clichés of print culture; it creates a McLuhanesque anti-environment that encourages readers to question their reading practices. Although the flow of thought from one quadrant to the next may be continuous, as in this example, at times the reader is forced to find connections or live in the gap.

349

But Ibsenist theatre has restricted itself to prose which retrieves ordinary speech.

350

It has done so by imitation of motion pictures, where dialogue ceases to be probe but is a quotation of dialogue.

351

Reacting against Ibsenist theatre, Arnaud in the 1930's insisted that speeches in the theatre of cruelty he calls for in The Theatre and its Double must be like like the speeches heard in a dream, i.e. archetypal.

352

Though his book and other writings about theatre have been of great influence because what he says is verbal envelope, he nevertheless failed to see that theatre dialogue must be based on verbal surround or go into discard.

Facing page:
Watson's "quadrant" typescript draft of *From Cliché to Archetype* (95-95)

Published accounts of Watson and McLuhan's work on *From Cliché to Archetype* in this final stage rest on two assumptions: that when the two men sat down in Toronto in the fall of 1968 to complete the book, McLuhan ignored the work Watson had done and started anew, and that Watson's voice and his contribution are marginalized in the published text. McLuhan biographer Philip Marchand, for example, writes:

> When [McLuhan and Watson] sat down to dictate the book to Margaret Stewart . . . they immediately ran into trouble. McLuhan did most of the dictating and ignored almost every idea that had developed in the dialogues with Watson, reverting to his original thoughts on the subject. Watson was not sure whether McLuhan actually forgot what they had talked about or whether he was simply ignoring their joint conversations. Given McLuhan's state of mind at the time — his loss of memory [following brain surgery] and the tormented state of his nervous system — either possibility was likely. (219)

At least two related factors contribute to this view: attempts by Viking Press to remove Watson's name from the title page, which ultimately resulted in a change of authorship, from McLuhan *and* Watson to McLuhan *with* Watson; and Watson's own published statements that McLuhan had transformed their dialogue into a monologue.[31] That Viking wanted to remove Watson's name from the title page of *From Cliché to Archetype* should not surprise: in the late 1960s, McLuhan's fame was such that a co-author seemed more a nuisance than a marketing opportunity. Given the inability of the two men to develop long-term collaborative strategies, the breakdown of their dialogue in 1968–69, while profoundly disappointing to both men, also seems unsurprising.

Both were bitterly disappointed by the failure of *From Cliché to Archetype* to live up to expectations. While it is tempting to interpret Watson's next play, *Let's Murder Clytemnestra According to the Principles of Marshall McLuhan*, which premiered at Studio Theatre on November 21, 1969, as a critique of — if not an outright attack on — McLuhan, that temptation should be resisted. Watson chose to collaborate with McLuhan because he believed he had something to learn from his co-author; in each play following *Cockcrow and the Gulls* — that is, from *Corporal Adam* and *Wail* to *DIP* and *Let's Murder Clytemnestra* — Watson put McLuhan's thinking to the test; in one way or another, each was written "according to the principles of Marshall McLuhan." Readers seeking to understand Watson's engagement with McLuhan's work might want to test the argument Stan Dragland has made concerning Watson. Confronted by the title page of *From Cliché to Archetype* — "Marshall McLuhan with Wilfred Watson" — Dragland asks:

> 'With.' What does that mean? McLuhan has the whole reputation, even now. . . . Who knows about Wilfred Watson, his poems, his plays, his stories? In the reputation sweepstakes, just a few. A few lucky readers know that Watson could think and write circles around Marshall McLuhan — not that it makes sense to speak of thinking and writing so. . . . (5)[32]

Those reading Watson's plays and poetry in relation to his journals, notebooks, and correspondence will find the experience richly rewarding and will recognize, as Paul Tiessen has, that the playwright/poet went on engaging with McLuhan's thinking long after he wrote *Let's Murder Clytemnestra*. This engagement continued until Watson's death, but it was particularly intense during the mid-1970s to the early 1980s, spurred by the facts that he was deeply involved with Sheila Watson and Fred Flahiff in planning a volume of essays on McLuhan they were editing and for which he had suggested the title *Reconnaissances*,[33] and that he did contribute a piece on "McLuhan's Wordplay" to the *The Canadian Forum*. Such readers will also detect Watson's probing of McLuhan's ideas in many of his new number-grid poems such as "putting one environment around another" and "Edvard Munch paints the High Level bridge."

STUDIO THEATRE
Presents It's Second Major Production For 69-70
Let's Murder Clytemnestra According To The Principles Of Marshall McLuhan
by Wilfred Watson
November 21 to November 29
One Free Student Ticket Available On I.D. Card
Tickets available November 17 between 9 a.m. and 4 p.m. in Room 312, Corbett Hall

Poster announcing *Let's Murder Clytemnestra According to the Principles of Marshall McLuhan* (95-639)

I think of visual space as being the space into which we write, paint pictures, build monuments; and of auditory space as the space into which we perform

MACHINE

THE

the blur

machine

blur

BLUR

machine

BLUR

the

MACHINE

the

the blur machine

Previous spread: On one of several visits Daphne Marlatt made to the Watsons, she and Wilfred "quarreled" over his "theory of film as an over-rated art." Out of the quarrel came an aphorism and a series of paired drawings. The aphorism: "motion picture finds a way to set into motion the world the painter succeeds in arresting in silence" (91-263 May 11 1981). The drawings: Marlatt with "machine-blue eyes" (91-263 May 13 1981) opposite representations of "the blur machine" (91-263).

Number-Grid Verse

Some eight months before his retirement from the University of Alberta, Watson invented a prosody he termed number-grid verse; the first number-grid poem in his journal appears on January 5, 1976. Its genesis lay in the haiku, but where the Japanese form counted syllables, Watson counted words. By laying down a vertical grid of numbers from 1 to 9, and slotting one word on each side of numbers 1 through 8, and a single word to the right of number 9, he arrived at seventeen words. The numbers, he explained, allow the reader to recognize "the principle of counting" which structures the poem and introduce a "slight asymmetry" in which the words on either side of the number are almost balanced but there "is a slight pressure in the second set to make them fit the second grid." "[R]ead aloud, the grids act as a notation indicating this asymmetry and pressure" ("NGV as notation" ix–x). The archive contains hundreds of number-grid verse poems, most unpublished.

He promptly tested his system by writing a series of "pseudo-haikus," " which he called "honkus," using his grid (91-219 Feb 16 1976). And he started playing around. He wrote "extended" honkus by repeating the grid or variations on it. He arranged the grid with some lines right justified, others centred, and the number 9 left justified, and he slotted words into the grid in such a way that their visual position on the page subtly underlined assonance and vowel patterns — what he called "tonal ligatures" (91-231 Jan 1 1978). By April 1976 he was writing poems with double and triple grids, which he stacked for multiple voices and which he often used contrapuntally. He experimented with the use of phrases rather than single words in each of the slots and with the silences of empty slots. In the purely formal regularity of the grid, he had discovered a remarkable flexibility.

Number-grid poetry addressed three of Watson's persistent concerns. We have noted that in *The Sorrowful Canadians* he thought he had achieved "the recognition factor" he sought. Number-grid verse took this a step further: "this new number grid logo is functional topologically, as well as working qua logo. The number grid not only functions on the page, but it also functions in the air: it is both visual, and auricular. It de-clichés both the look of verse but also the language itself" (91-234 Aug 28 1978).

His second concern was with auditory space and the way in which the "purely formal" "invariable" of the number grid could enable performance of the poem (91-221 July 8 1976). While the arrangement of stacked grids for multi-voice poems invites an analogy with a musical score, he was adamant that no such tight link existed between the "poem as seen on the page" and "the poem as heard" in performance. "The poem on

Number-grid verse as both visual and auditory (91-238)

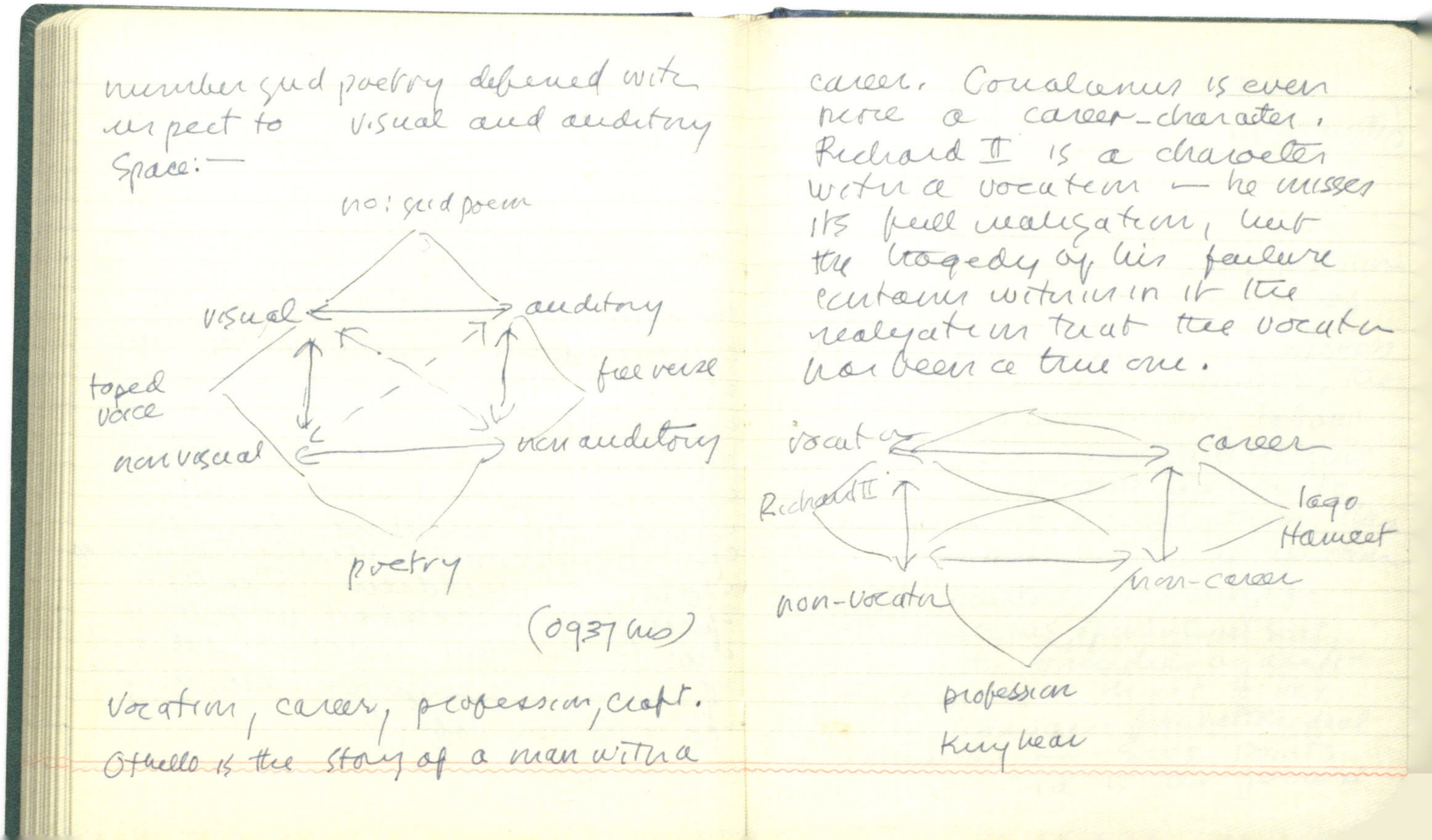

Below:
A dramatic presentation of poems from *I Begin with Counting* on the occasion of its 1978 publication

Facing page:
"re the blue jays of april fifteen" (*I Begin with Counting*)

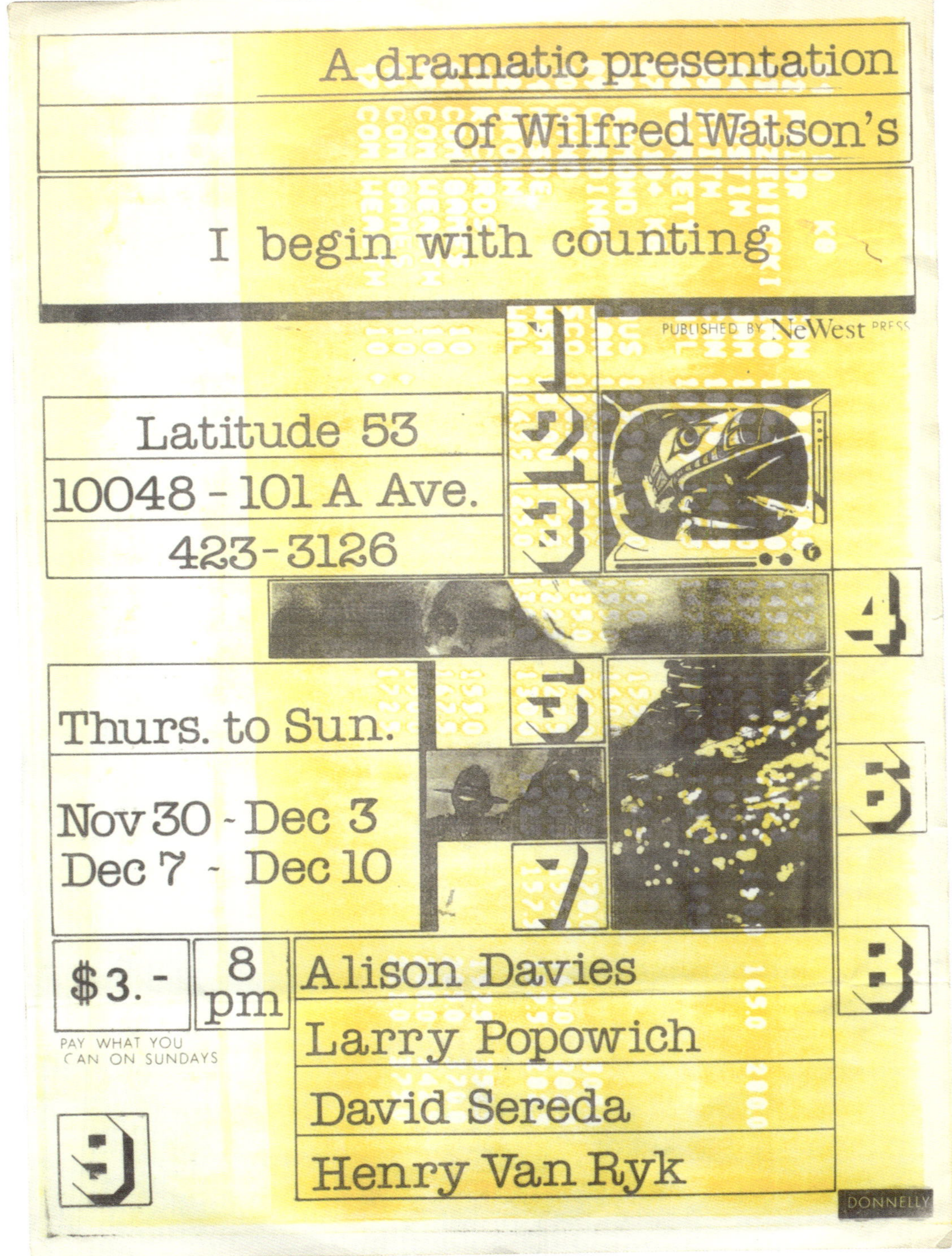

the women of trachis

1 (deianira
figures 1 at
contra) 2
the 2 clothes-line
(burning) 3 a
3
contingent 4 matter
in 4 a
(burning) 5
necessary 5 form
6 (burning)
the 6 traditional
7 (the
bond 7 is
shirt 8 of
nostalgia 8 o
9 nessus)
9 heraklitos

heraklitos 1 heraklitos
figures 1 at
heraklitos 2 I
the 2 clothes-line
know 3 all
3
4 about
shit, 4 heraklitos
5 you
count 5 no
can't 6 step
woman 6 happy
into 7 the
until 7 she
same 8 death
8 is
9 twice
9 dead

re the blue jays of april fifteen

kyrie 1 kyrie
blue 1 jay
kyrie 2 crying
blue 2 jay
crying 3 crying
blue 3 jay
crying 4
kyrie 4
crying 5 crying
kyrie 5 kyrie
crying 6
kyrie 6
kyrie 7 kyrie
jay 7 blue
kyrie 8
jay 8
9 crying
9 eleison

waking 1 up
1
years 2 ago
2
in 3 a
3
now 4
4
shipyard 5
and 5 the
6
tomorrowing 6
7
crashing 7 through
and 8
transparent 8
9 welders
9 wet

the page isn't simply a notation for the poem vibrating in the air. The performed poem is a **transformation** of the seen poem," a transformation from "visual" to "auditory" or "actor's space" ("Notation" x, xii, xiv). Watson's journals for these years frequently probe the distinction between visual and auditory space, attempting to push beyond McLuhan's concepts. He returned in these years to McLuhan's notions of visual and auditory space more frequently than to any of his other ideas, modifying them to foreground the creative artist and performance:

> McLuhan supposed visual space to be the space men think in and auditory space to be the space we live in. I think of visual space as being the space into which we write, paint pictures, build monuments; and of auditory space as the space into which we perform — not quite the same

> thing as the space we live in, which I think of as the aggregate (*in toto*, virtually unthinkable) of all the spaces we deal with. (xiv)

Performances by actors[34] of the number-grid verse proved revelatory for actors, audience, and Watson himself; it is doubtful that anyone who heard the performance of a poem such as "re the blue jays of april fifteenth" ever forgot the way in which the counterpointing of "kyrie 1 kyrie" against "blue jay 1 blue jay" enacted and counterpointed the haunting and raucous call of the birds and the eternal petition of mankind, "*Kyrie*, May the Lord have mercy on us" (*Poems* 278–79). Those performances convinced Watson that the "auditory form changes from performance to performance" and that the "total poem, its poetry," lay neither in its visual nor its auditory form but in its "transformations" from the visual to the auditory ("Notation" xiv). He had achieved his long-desired synthesis of poetry and play, of script transformed into performance, many performances.

Watson's third persistent concern, which he felt number-grid verse addressed, was the creation of a verse form that could, with use, become indigenous, which is to say, "a form which has been practiced by the natives of a place for a number of generations" (91-236 Jan 2 1979). "To invent a new form is to invent a new literature," he observed: "This is what Emily Carr does. She gives us a new way of looking at the deforestation of B.C. not a new B.C. or a new forest" (91-246 Sept 1 1981). He understood the number grid as a new way of looking at English metrics, a way that did not involve breaking up traditional forms, as did American free verse. What his number grids do is count, as does metrical verse, but they count differently and with more flexibility. Number-grid verse, he held, "preserves" traditional metrics "by creating an order akin as order to the order traditional metrics pursued" at the same time as it extends them (91-221 July 8 1976). Which is to say, perhaps, that number-grid verse is both radically "new" and fundamentally conservative. Watson believed that he had achieved with his new prosody a form that could be used to develop a Canadian verse "radically (because formally) distinct from North American vers libre" with its view of language "as a raw material to be shattered and reshaped." Language, as in his youth, remained sacred: "To me language is the living body of humanity, a body of fate which can be identified with, but not revamped or transformed" (91-220 Apr 24 1976; 91-234 Sept 11 1978).

Man exteriorizes his needs,
in his technologies.
This is a world-destroying
process; and art is the
attempt to heal the trauma
caused by technological
innovation

Drawing made while working on "Blancnoir" (91-230)

Gramsci x 3

Within six months of devising his number grids, Watson was thinking about how to use them in the theatre. He had not been able to complete to his satisfaction the plays he was writing at the time. He had been working for some time, and would continue working for at least another five years, on a play that he titled, variously, "The White Rhodesians" or "Blancnoir" and that he ultimately judged a confidence-sapping failure (91-305 draft letter to Shirley Neuman Feb 5 1983). A second effort, "The Judgment: After Kafka," went little better. It was not to these works but to a paraphrase of Sophocles that he turned to test the feasibility of using number-grid verse in playwriting. He conceived of "The Women of Trachis" as a "pilot study" in the use of number-grid verse in drama (91-223 Nov 14 1976) and worked on the play over the next two years, focusing on the Dejanira/Iole/Herakles triangle. He hoped that Gordon Peacock would direct it; he didn't.

Instead Watson found the subject for the last of his major works in twentieth-century politics. After reading James Joll's *Gramsci*, on March 20, 1978 he projected a play about the Italian Communist revolutionary. Sheila Watson encouraged him and the next day borrowed for him Guiseppe Fiore's *Antonio Gramsci.* Fiori's phrase, adapted, "the long calvary of Nino Gramsci" (*Plays* 559), became the structural pivot of *Gramsci x 3*. By May 1978 he had a completed script of "The Young Officer from Cagliari," initially projected as the third and final act (it ultimately became the first act). Watson was clear that, despite his source material, he was writing "myth" and allegory, not documentary.

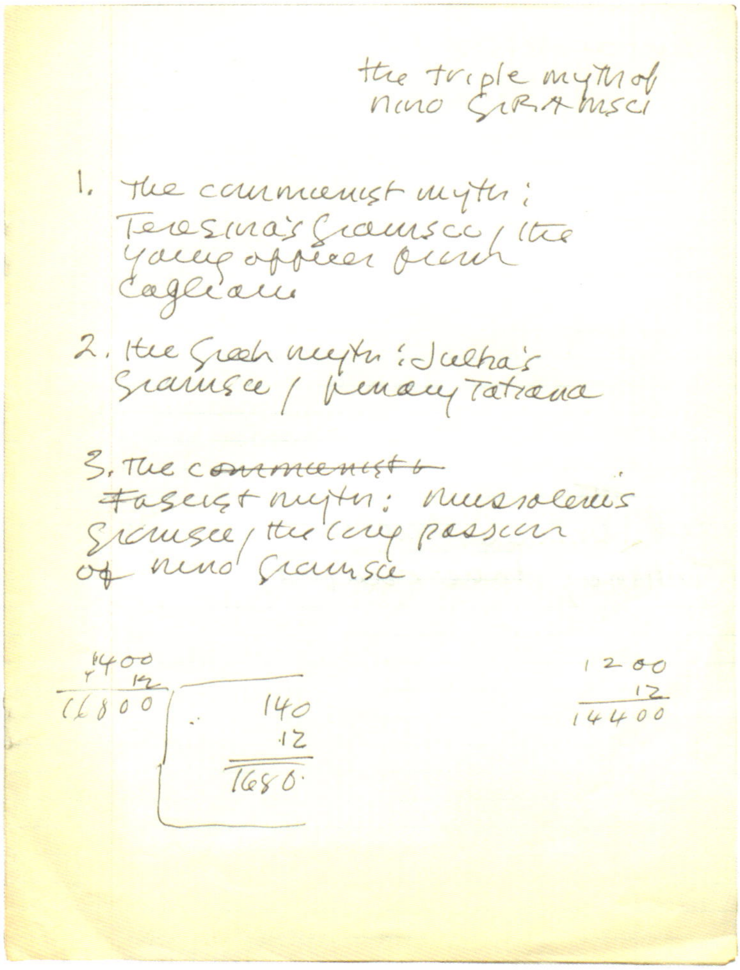

Left:
The myths of Gramsci (95-116)

Facing page:
Schema for "characterizations as masks of power" (95-02)

He signalled this point immediately in "The Young Officer" by creating an entirely fictional character, Teresina, to be Gramsci's niece who shares his frail build and big hair and who is waiting with her family for the release of the long-imprisoned revolutionary. Teresina, he wrote, is "invented so that the other roles in this dramatic experiment could be approached thru her eyes as myth, not as the simulations of documentary. The falsifications of documentary are dogmatic, those of myth are really questions" (95-02). "The Young Officer from Cagliari" announces Gramsci's death and was written quickly. Watson appears to have had more difficulty deciding how to dramatize the revolutionary's life.

He began to get a sense of the direction of his last two plays/acts when he hazarded that, "Perhaps the Xn truth is this: that death on the cross is demanded of us, one and all. We seek to survive . . . to escape being destroyed. We see ourselves as victims when what we are is survivors, miserable and unable to sacrifice a little finger for the good of . . . " (Watson's ellipsis; 91-236 Jan 6 1979). One of his schematizations of his characters outlines their sacrifices, with Mussolini and Gramsci at opposite ends of the spectrum: Gramsci "sacrifices himself for the Communist cause" and "re-invent[s] self-sacrifice" whereas "Mussolini sees the truth but won't sacrifice himself to it so remaining an opportunist" (95-02; *Plays* 433).

chorus as masks of power

Julka as a communist sees GRAMSCI as sacrificing communism to the lost cause of communism in Fascist Italy

Tatiana wants to sacrifice herself to preventing Gramsci from sacrificing himself to lost cause communism and encouraging him to re-think the communist theme under the sting of Mussolini's opportunism

Mussolini sees the truth but won't sacrifice himself to it so remains an opportunist

GRAMSCI ↓ becomes less a revolutionary and more and more someone who sacrifices himself for the communist cause which Mussolini thinks superseded by Fascist thought

Watson arrived at the structure of *Gramsci* some ten months after this return to the allegory of the Crucifixion: "Gramsci: portrait of Gramsci as his niece, part one. / Portrait of Gramsci with Tatiana. / Portrait of Gramsci as the disciple that Jesus loved" (91-239 Oct 16 1979). However, he worked on other things until the beginning of 1981, when he outlined for himself the material, psychological, technological, sociological, and "magical or spiritual" allegories of the play (91-275 Aug 7 1981) before setting it aside to prepare *Mass on Cow Back* and "NGV as notation." Only in January 1982 did he return to the play. Over the next months he thought hard about the function of the chorus in *Gramsci*. He recollected his Paris attendance at the Obey adaptation of the *Oresteia* (91-286) and claimed to have taken his "inspiration" for the chorus from a broadcast performance by The Four Horsemen: "I came to an understanding of the chorus by reversing the traditional account of how characterization arose out of the Greek chorus: if multi-consciousness, then the chorus develops free characterization, or in response to the need for the multi-autobiographical role" (91-297 copy of letter to bpNichol Sept 8 1982).

3612 place road, Nanaimo, bc
V9T 1M8

September 8, 1982

dear bp

A lone black brant goose paraded before the house this time yesterday morning, very ominous. When we returned from circum-footing the spit, the O P E N L E T T E R

no
tay
syun

was in the mailbox. I like it, everything about it, conception, execution, structuring and texture; the cover is magnificently sensual, sensuously magnificent, and vice-versa. I'm conceitedly vain and proud to be included in it. I absolutely endorse and approve the design of the text of my piece: you need have no fear about my 'first sentences'. They could have been black lettered without much damage, but I intended them to be done as in fact they have been —I adopted this pointing from George Price's book on Kierkegaard. Thank you. I will make a point of attending the 4 horsemen when they come to nanaimo. I enjoyed very much the broadcast by them of earlier this summer, so much so that the four horsemen have become the inspiration of choruses I'm using in the second and third parts of Gramsci, which is now within sight of a completion. I don't think of these choruses as decoration; in fact, I came to an understanding of the chorus by reversing the traditional account of how characterization arose out of the Greek chorus; if multi-consciousness, then the chorus develops from characterization, or in response to the need for the multi-autobiographical role.

Before the brant goose came the first cc of Mass on cowback. Irma Sommerfeld, whose profile travestied precedes the benedictus section, is coming here on friday from edmonton and bringing with her additional copies, one of which I'll send on to you. I've stolen part of NGV as notation, or more correctly encouraged S. Longspoon to steal it, as preface, and if as I hope isn't the case, this theft is distasteful to you, I can only plead that it is functional and that everything in the book, and the book itself flows from it.

Facing page:
Gramsci, Oresteia, and The Four Horsemen; Watson to bpNichol, Sept 8 1982 (95-02)

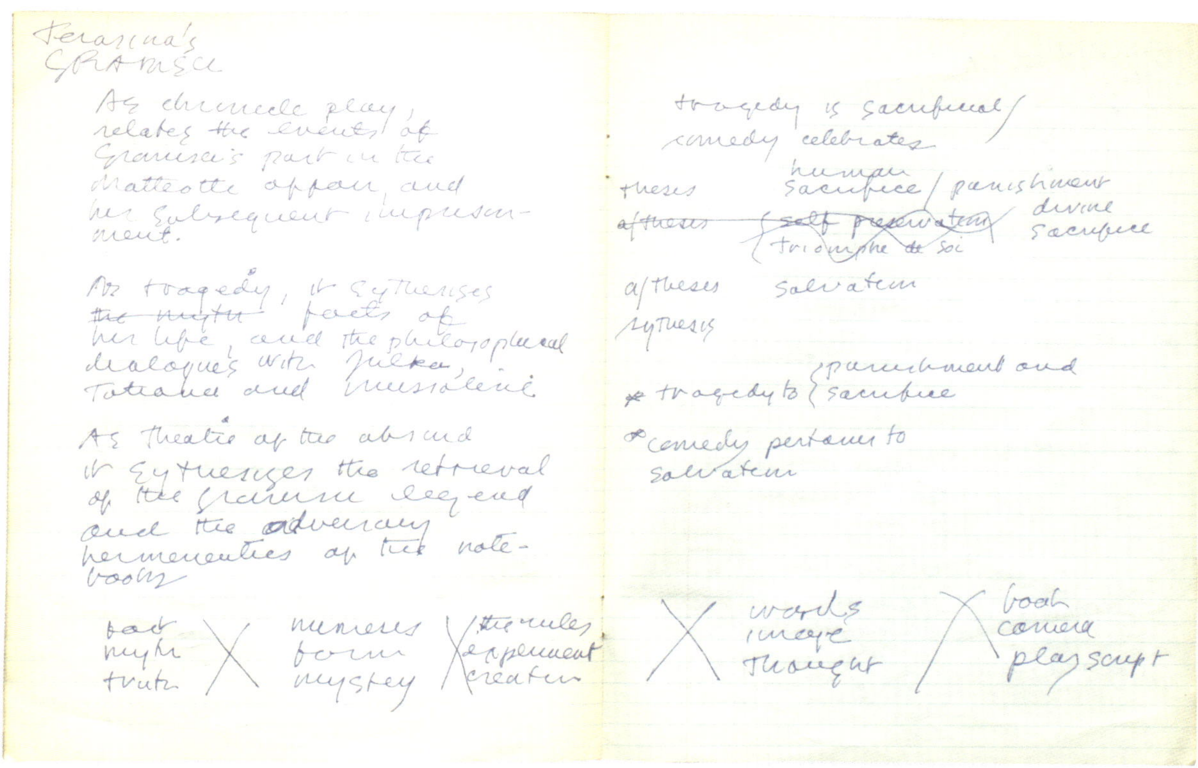

Perassina's
GRAMSCI

As chronicle play, relates the events of Gramsci's part in the Matteotti affair and his subsequent imprisonment.

As tragedy, it synthesises ~~the myth~~ facts of his life, and the philosophical dialogues with Julka, Tatiana and Mussolini.

As theatre of the absurd it synthesises the retrieval of the Gramsci legend and the adversary hermeneutics of the notebooks

fact / myth / truth X numbers / form / mystery X the rules / experiment / creation

tragedy is sacrificial / comedy celebrates

theses — human sacrifice / punishment — divine sacrifice

antitheses — ~~self preservation~~ / triomphe de soi

antitheses — salvation

synthesis

* tragedy to { punishment and sacrifice

* comedy pertains to salvation

X words / image / thought X book / camera / playscript

Below:
Gramsci as chronicle, tragedy, and theatre of the absurd (95-02)

By February 1982 he had decided that *Gramsci 3* would take "the form of . . . a chaconne or passacaglia, variations . . . on a ground bass, founded on the stations of the cross, as listed in 'Returning to Square One'" in *I Begin with Counting*, that is, in reverse order (91-303 Feb 4 1982). Numerous chronologies attest to the care with which he worked out the analogies between the Stations of the Cross and the details of Gramsci's imprisonment. Despite the Christian allegory and the theatrical and moving ritual of the recitation of the Stations of the Cross, however, Watson's Passion play turned in the direction of the tragically absurd: in the workbook in which he enumerates Gramsci's Stations of the Cross, he also writes that the "synthesis of myth/meme and logos/philosophical dialogue equals tragic farce/theatre of the absurd" (91-512). *Gramsci* is replete with "logos/philosophical dialogue," not only in the debate between Gramsci and his wife in the second act/play, but also in his conception that the play's "caricatures" (as he called his characters) were masks of 20C corporate power, viz, democratic capitalism, communism, fascism and totalitarianism, and as such have, like the fields of force they represent, reference to money as a global language which ~~operates as~~ articulates fact, myth, and truth, i.e. statistically, semantically, and metaphysically. (95-02)

His notebooks from the years in which he works on *Gramsci* turn around reflections on capital, the function of money, the nature of violence, his reading of Sorel, his reassessment of McLuhan. And, of course, as soon as he gave the names of Scalpel, Urine-bottle, and Castor-oil to the doctors tending Gramsci unto death, he stepped into the world of tragic farce he had first entered when he gave to his Everyman the name Cockcrow.

As in *Cockcrow,* redemption comes through transfiguration, enacted in ritual. It is in the months when he begins to work intensively on *Gramsci*, and particularly with the Stations of the Cross, that his ongoing reassessment of McLuhan leads to one of Watson's clearest articulations of his understanding of the function of the artist. "The great artists, Dante, Shakespeare, Joyce, MM thought, were concerned to adjust the minds of their contemporaries to the disorder of relationships caused by new technologies," he begins. In his "re-phrasing of the idea," via Wyndham Lewis's idea of the "wild body" and the "magical body":

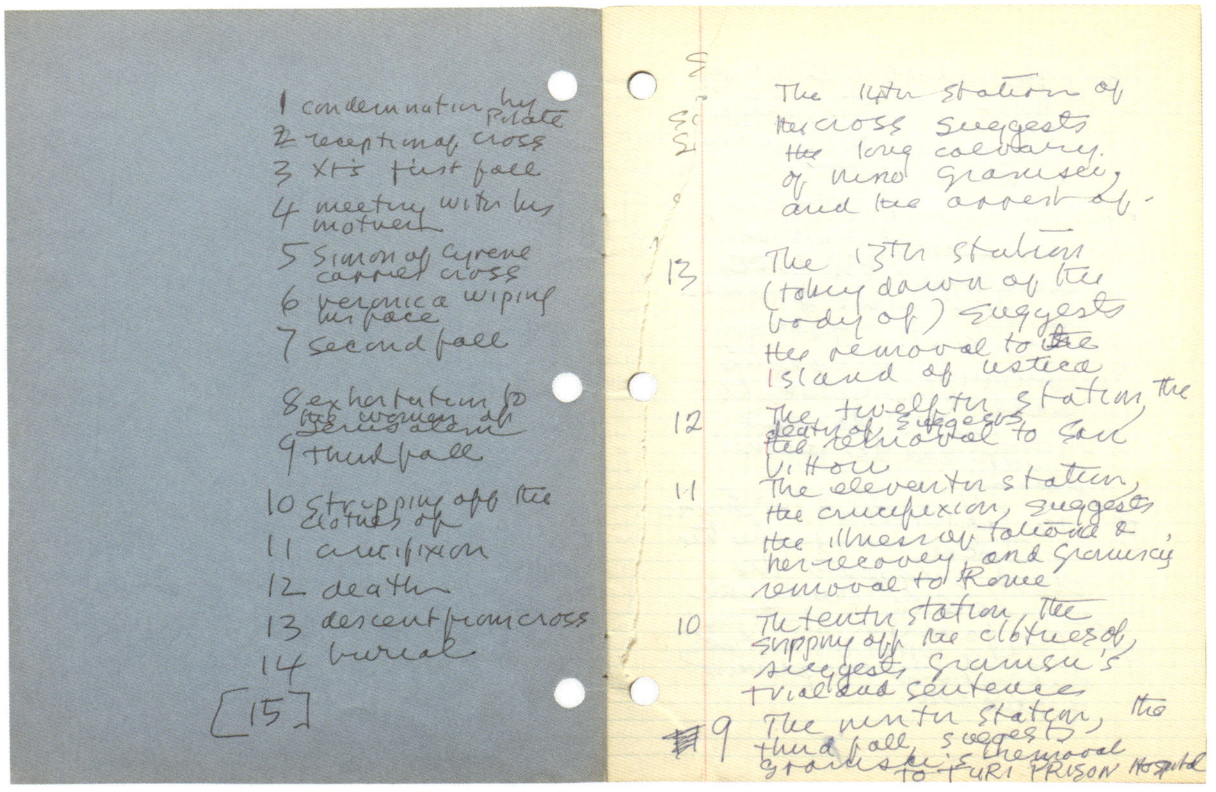
1 condemnation by Pilate
2 reception of cross
3 Xt's first fall
4 meeting with his mother
5 Simon of Cyrene carries cross
6 Veronica wiping his face
7 second fall
8 exhortation to the women of Jerusalem
9 third fall
10 stripping off the clothes of
11 crucifixion
12 death
13 descent from cross
14 burial
[15]

The 14th station of the cross suggests the long calvary of Nino Gramsci, and the arrest of -
13 The 13th station (taking down of the body of) suggests the removal to the Island of Ustica
12 The twelfth station, the death of, suggests the removal to San Vittore
11 The eleventh station, the crucifixion, suggests the illness of Tatiana & her recovery, and Gramsci's removal to Rome
10 The tenth station, the stripping off the clothes of, suggests Gramsci's trial and sentence
9 The ninth station, the third fall, suggests the removal to TURI PRISON Hospital

One of Watson's several charts of parallels between the Crucifixion and the imprisonment of Gramsci (95-512)

STUDIO THEATRE MARCH 27 - APRIL 5

University of Alberta – Box office 432 2495 • WARNING: Nudity and violence in some scenes of the play

GRAMSCI

A WORLD PREMIERE

X 3

Written by

WILFRED WATSON

Directed by

THOMAS PEACOCKE

One of a series of posters for the production of *Gramsci x 3* (95-OS3-641)

> Man exteriorizes his needs, in his technologies. This is a world-destroying process; and art is the attempt to heal the trauma caused by technological innovation, to reconcile the wild body of animal technologies with the magical body of human technologies. Art is redemptive, attempts to be so, though the exteriorization of needs which is man's hubris and fatal aboriginal sin makes redemption possible only by denying his human nature. (91-287 Apr 7[?] 1982)

Here we arrive at a deeper truth of Watson's lifelong return to an allegory of the Crucifixion as birth. The allegory figures forth the intersubjectivity of God's gift to humankind, and, because the ritual that "enacts" it involves author, actors, and audience in co-creating its meaning, the play "transfigures" experience into a redemptive art. This is the religion of art as redemption that Watson discovered for himself, and this is the work of the "thinking heart" that led him to understand *Cockcrow* as an allegory of the artist and *Gramsci* as "an allegory about theatre as a revolutionary art" (*Plays* 433).

Gramsci x 3 was published in 1983. This marked the first time that Watson had published a play before it was performed; it also marked the first time he had an agreement with a publisher in advance of completing a work. The agreement included a date for submission, and he didn't have time to complete the retranscription of all the dialogue into number-grid verse. Looking at the prose of some dialogue, the poetic lines of other dialogue, and the number-grid verse of the most fully achieved passages, we can begin to understand something of his compositional process.

Thomas Peacocke directed *Gramsci x 3* for Studio Theatre in March 1986 to good reviews. Wilfred Watson attended the rehearsals and the opening days of the run. It was the last production of one of his plays during his lifetime. He died in March 1998, two months after Sheila Watson's death and a month short of his eighty-seventh birthday.

A life of prayer and
worship seems selfish
compared to the exchange
of energies such a
dialogue implies

Facing page:
Drawing by Wilfred Watson of Sheila Watson, inserted in April 2–June 19 1961 notebook (91-62)

Presences; Publication

In the epigraph with which we began this introduction to Wilfred Watson's archive, we saw him in 1979 thinking about his literary estate. Aged sixty-eight, he had a reputation as an avant-garde playwright, but it had been a decade since a play of his had seen performance. He had published three volumes of poetry, but they had received less attention than he had hoped. The literary papers for which he wanted to find a home contained tens of thousands of pages of unpublished work. Enter Sheila Watson. Asked if she had thought about arranging a depository for her own papers, she answered succinctly, "Wilfred's first."

Sheila Watson is a significant presence in the archive, especially in the correspondence between her and Wilfred Watson and in his journals. We have noted Watson in his notebooks and journals, as well as in his plays and poetry, in ongoing dialogue with Shakespeare, with Gabriel Marcel during the 1950s, with McLuhan from the late 1950s. Many other figures to whom we have been able to give less attention inhabit his thoughts and probes. They include Northrop Frye, whose *Anatomy of Criticism* Watson read immediately on its appearance. It made him anxious and his notebooks from the 1950s, long before he and McLuhan began to work together, are full

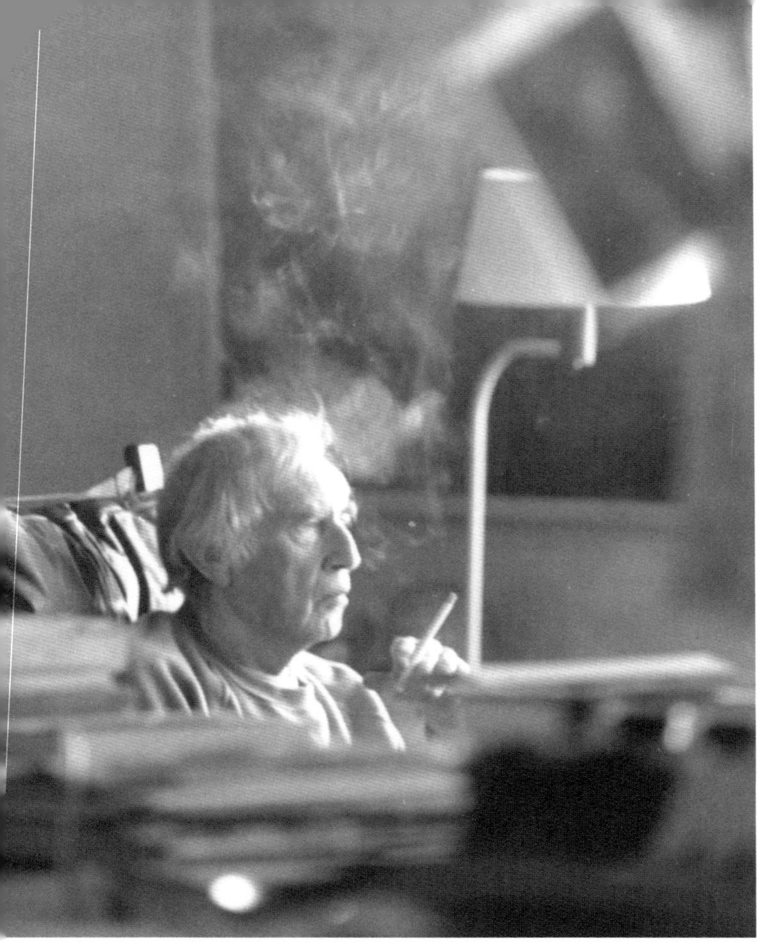

Wilfred Watson, 1986, from a series of photographs by Jorge Frascara, one of which was used on the cover of *Poems* (95-24-14)

of questions and hypotheses about archetypes and archetypal criticism, many of which would find their way, directly or indirectly, into his collaboration with McLuhan. They have much to add to the important work undertaken by Richard Cavell and, more recently, Bruce Powe about Frye and McLuhan in relation to one another. From 1955, when Watson read the last two volumes of *The Human Age*, he returned very frequently to the ideas of Wyndham Lewis; there is much in his papers with which to enlarge the understanding of his relationship to Vorticism that Gregory Betts has begun to sketch. Canadian authors appear again and again. He greets Irving Layton, for example, with scathing contempt; Alice Munro he finds predictable; he proves generous and admiring toward figures such as Helen Humphries, bpNichol, Robert Kroetsch, Marian Engel, and Sylvia Fraser. Sheila Watson inhabits the archive from first to last. She is "swp" (short for "shuswap" and then for "Sheila white pelican") and late in life she is "wong." Watson reports her witticisms, her questions, and her astute judgement. He records her doings. He writes her poetry. Some seven months after the couple had moved to Nanaimo, on the occasion of their thirty-ninth wedding anniversary, he wrote:

> This marriage has been like a M-M-ian dialogue, a debate about the irony and wonder of things, with insights, pattern-recognitions, break thrus, and flytings. The last few months, with their tide water interfaces, have revived this dialogue. A life of prayer and worship seems selfish compared to the exchange of energies such a dialogue implies. (91-243a Dec 29 1980)

The "dialogue" Watson sought his entire life he found most reliably across the kitchen table, in the person of Sheila Doherty Watson.

He also found in her an unshakable loyalty to his writing. Just as she had sent his work to Faber and Faber, published him in *white pelican*, and now pushed to have arrangements made for his literary archive, so Sheila Watson was a moving force behind the significant publication of his work in the 1980s. George Melnyk at NeWest Press had enthusiastically brought out *I Begin with Counting* in 1978. The book got attention, but publishers weren't beating down Watson's door. It was Sheila Watson who said to Longspoon Press, "Publish Wilfred." Longspoon did, beginning with a second collection of number-grid verse, *Mass on Cow Back* (1982), and with *Gramsci x 3* (1983).

But a more ambitious effort seemed necessary if readers were to understand the scope and coherence of Watson's *oeuvre*. Longspoon and NeWest Presses undertook to co-publish first *Poems: Collected/Unpublished/New* (1987), then *Plays at the Iron Bridge* (1989). Sheila Watson undertook the immense task of editing *Poems*, though she refused to let her name appear on the volume. Working with Wilfred Watson, she assembled not only the previously published work but also a large body of unpublished poetry. With *Plays at the Iron Bridge*, Watson took the decision to include five of his full-length plays, from *Cockcrow* to *Gramsci*, including four plays produced at Studio Theatre and one, *Another Bloody Page from Plutarch*, that had never been produced. Only *Gramsci x 3* had seen previous publication. Last of all, NeWest published *The Baie Comeau Angel and Other Stories* (1993). That collection opened with two early stories, "The Lice" (a well-known allegory of the artist) and "Four Times Canada Is Four"; it centred on "The Girl Who Lived in a Glass Box," a story Watson had written early in the 1960s and rediscovered in 1980 when culling his papers prior to his last move; and it concluded with two late stories.

These volumes are very far from "collected" in the sense of including all the work an author thinks worth preserving. But they do trace a trajectory from Watson's earliest successful work in a genre to his latest. They allow a reader to see something of how his writing developed over a period of nearly fifty years, to appreciate something of its inventiveness, and to begin to understand its coherence and its major preoccupations. They float, as it were, atop the vast body of work in Watson's literary archive.

The archive offers significant opportunities to deepen our discussions of topics such as Canadian Vorticism, cultural nationalism, Canadian theatre history, communication and media theory, and the work of Marshall McLuhan. It reveals how deeply allegorical and emblematic all Watson's thought and work is. It enables an understanding of the eclecticism from which he probes his own preoccupations and the preoccupations of his contemporaries and his time, and of his complex relationship to literary tradition and to Canadian literature. It offers hundreds of glimpses of how he transfigures the "anti-poetic" material of the life and concerns he found around him by means of allegory, satire, playfulness, and the recognitions of the "thinking heart." -/-

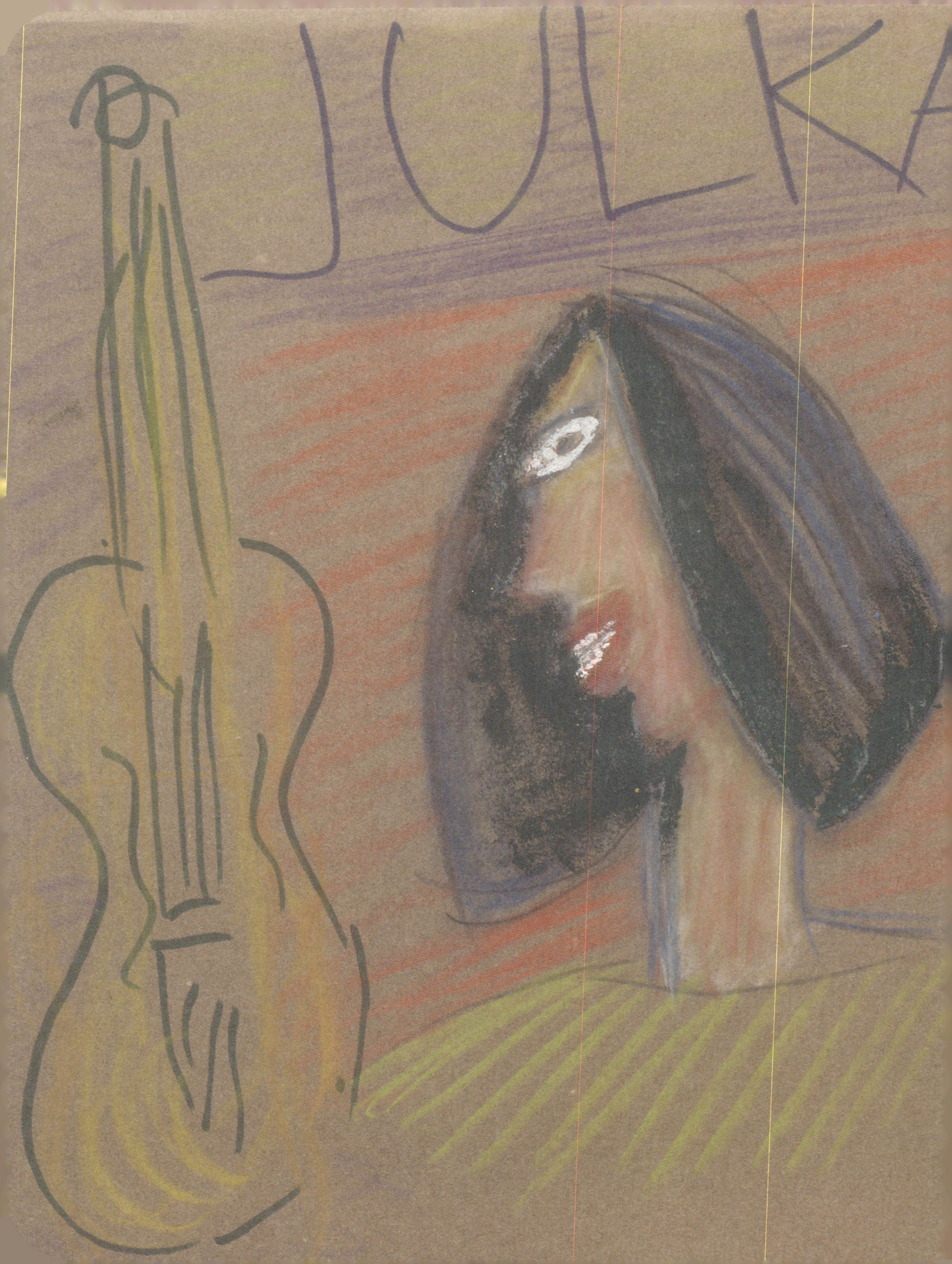
JULKA

Facing page:
The artist; a drawing of Gramsci's wife, Julka, with her violin (95-292)

Notes

1 All references to the Wilfred Watson Fonds are identified by the last two digits of the accession year and the file number. Thus 91-2 refers to accession 1991-117-folder 2; 95-3 refers to accession 1995-131-folder 3 and so on. For photographs, however, the identification system in the archive makes it necessary to include the box number. Thus 95-24-16 refers to accession 1995-131, box 24, folder 16.

2 All references to the Sheila Watson Fonds will be identified as SW followed by the folder number. The accession number is always 2006 01.

3 In the fall of 1953 Watson submitted poems to *Crux Magazine, Northern Review Press, Poetry Magazine (Chicago), Beloit Poetry Journal, The Wind and the Rain, Fiddlehead,* and *Queen's Quarterly.* He may also have submitted poems to *The Paris Review* at this time: the finding aid for the Watson archive indicates that folder 91-448, which includes typescripts of poems he submitted for publication in 1953, also included an envelope (since lost) postmarked Stanford. Donald Hall, editor of the *Paris Review,* was a Creative Writing Fellow at Stanford University in 1953–54. He knew enough of Watson's work by early 1955 that the latter felt confident in asking him to serve as a reference for his Overseas Fellowship. A draft letter dated August 3, 1953, from Watson to Ann Taylor, editor at McClelland and Stewart, offered her *Friday's Child* (91-367).

4 "Lines for the Twenty-fifth Anniversary of the Declaration of War, August 4, 1914," XIX.226 (Nov 1939): 256; "Compartments," XIX.230 (March 1940): 392; "Armed Merchantman," XX.233 (June 1940): 88.

5 *Contemporary Verse*, 35 (Summer 1951): 3–6 and 38 (Summer 1952): 18–19.

6 *Fiddlehead* 20 (Feb. 1954): 1.

7 *The London Magazine*, 28 (1955): 24–25; *The Paris Review*, 9 (Summer 1955): 95 and 10 (Fall 1955): 50–52.

8 Michael Roberts, ed., *The Faber Book of Modern Verse* (London: Faber and Faber, 1936), and *New Signatures: Poems by Several Hands*, collected by Michael Roberts (London: Hogarth P, 1932).

9 See ms. draft, "The birth of tom horror" (91-117), the June 18, 1956 notebook entry (91-17), a draft biographical note (91-369), and Sheila Watson to T.S. Eliot, draft letter (SW-570).

10 Late in life, Watson often misremembered the date of his arrival in Canada as 1926, when he was fifteen. The passenger manifest for the *Melita*, however, lists the entire family arriving from Southampton on July 10, 1925. Watson often errs by a year or two in dating events; we have found no evidence that he misremembers what happened.

11 Richard (Dick) Halhed and Elmer Hunt were Watson's "cell-mates at Chemainus" sawmill (91-311 Dec 18 1985). Halhed became an announcer and producer for the CBC (95-376).

12 Information from Watson's UBC transcript and from course descriptions in the *University of British Columbia Calendar 1941–42*. The honours thesis is in the archive (95-565).

13 Information about Watson's graduate work at the University of Toronto comes from his Faculty of Graduate Studies file and from the University of Toronto *Calendar* for 1945–46 to 1947–48. The remark about the course on the *Exeter Book* was made to Fred Flahiff, who reported it to Neuman.

14 A whiskeyjack (more commonly spelled *whisky jack*) is a jay. Watson's first six "Whiskeyjack" columns appeared in the following issues of *The New Trail*: XI.2–4 (1953); XII.2–4 (1954); "Wingfeathers" in XIII.2 (Summer 1955) and "Whiskeyjack in Montmartre" in XIII.4 (Winter 1955). Another column, "The Chipmunk," identifies him as "Whiskeyjack" in XIII.4 (Winter 1955). Consulted 9 June 2014 at http://peel.library.ualberta.ca/bibliography/9042.40.

15 Although the initial idea was that the two would exchange roles "to prevent readers from making an equation" (95-198 WW to SW, May 31 1958), this appears not to have happened, leaving Daniells playing the straight man. He was having fun by naming the voice of orthodox cultural nationalism Trueman. Albert Trueman became President of the University of Manitoba in 1945, one year before Daniells, Head of English there, left for UBC. From 1953 to 1957 Trueman chaired the National Film Board of Canada, and from 1957 to 1965 he served as the first Director of the Canada Council for the Arts.

16 Joyce Amelia Wontner (1934–2013), a Calgary student of early childhood education when Watson met her, began her career in Lake Louise but shortly moved back to Calgary where she taught until retirement. On Watson's initiative, the couple resumed their affair briefly in June 1959 and were in touch by mail over the summer (91-29 May 24, 31 and June 3 1959; SW-12 Aug 30 1959). In September 1959 he noted that he had "been thinking of marriage" to her and that he had

written her (91-30). Whatever proposal his letter conveyed, she had learned to refuse. There is no record in his papers that they had further contact beyond a congratulatory telegram (lost or misplaced in the archive) that she sent for the opening of *Cockcrow*. She never married.

Marcel argues that the act of giving all our energies to some purpose outside ourselves, without hope of receiving anything, "is essentially creative" and that the person carrying out such a sacrifice/dedication "most completely *is*, in the act of giving his life away" (I.165–66). He is speaking of martyrs and soldiers.

17 Beginning in the summer of 1957 the Watsons spent time together every summer and Christmas. They were reunited in the summer of 1961 when Sheila Watson took a position at the University of Alberta.

18 Published as "Blackberry Pickers of Vancouver Island," *Prism* (Winter 1961): 51–52.

19 Matthew, 13:46.

20 G.N.M. Tyrell, *Apparitions* (1943; London: Duckworth, rev. ed. 1953); and *The Nature of Human Personality* (N.Y.: Collier, 1954).

21 The fellowship, which was open to creative and performing artists and could be held in either France or Holland, was administered for Foreign Affairs by the Royal Society of Canada.

22 *Eschyle et l'Orestie* in the series Cahiers de la Compagnie Madeleine Renaud Jean-Louis Barrault (Paris: René Juillard, 1955) (91-596).

23 This list is derived from Sheila Watson's Paris journals (SW-3, 5, 6, 9).

24 Seven of these poems were published in *The Humanities Association Bulletin*, XIV (Fall 1963), and an eighth in *white pelican*, 1.1 (Winter 1971); the rest saw light only with the publication of *Poems* (1986).

25 Roy Campbell translated sections of Federico García Lorca's *Llanto por Ignacio Sánchez Mejías* (1935) in his *Lorca: An Appreciation of His Poetry* (Cambridge: Bowes & Bowes, 1952): 70–77. In the second section, every second line is the "hysterical refrain" (73) "At five in the afternoon"; in the third, variations of "I do not want to look at it!" begin or end stanzas.

26 "The Canadian Fact" was reprinted, with an introduction, in Whittaker's *Hot Thespian Action!* In his General Introduction Whittaker provides a valuable history both of Walterdale Theatre Associates and of amateur theatre in Edmonton.

27 The play received coverage in the *Globe and Mail* and *Toronto Star* as well as in Edmonton newspapers where it occasioned numerous letters to the editor and made an appearance in a Yardley Jones editorial cartoon.

28 All references to the Marshall McLuhan Fonds are to the Correspondence series and identified by volume and file number. Thus 40-27 refers to volume 40, file 27.

29 In a letter to William Toye dated February 8, 1987, Watson appears to confirm this timeline: "The idea for the book began with the title, which was agreed upon probably in mid-1963, when I was in Toronto to attend the performance of my play, *Corporal Adam*, at the Coach House Theatre; I stayed with the McLuhans for the twelve or so performances" (95-532).

30 C/A is one of the abbreviations Watson and McLuhan developed for *From Cliché to Archetype* in their correspondence.

31 Tiessen titles his essay on Watson's "encounter" with McLuhan, "Shall I Say, It Is Necessary to Restore the Dialogue."

32 Tiessen drew our attention to Dragland's comment; see his "Wilfred Watson, Playwright."

33 Flahiff and Watson, unable to agree about some of the contributions, passed their editorship on to Shirley Neuman and David Staines, who also proved unable to achieve the collection; it was never published.

34 Thomas Peacocke, Gwynyth Walsh, Christopher Lewis, and William Johnston gave the first public performance of number-grid verse in Edmonton in May 1979. In November 1979 Watson attended performances at Latitude 53 Gallery in Edmonton of "I Begin with Counting" by Alison Davies, Larry Popowich, David Sereda, and Henry van Ryk.

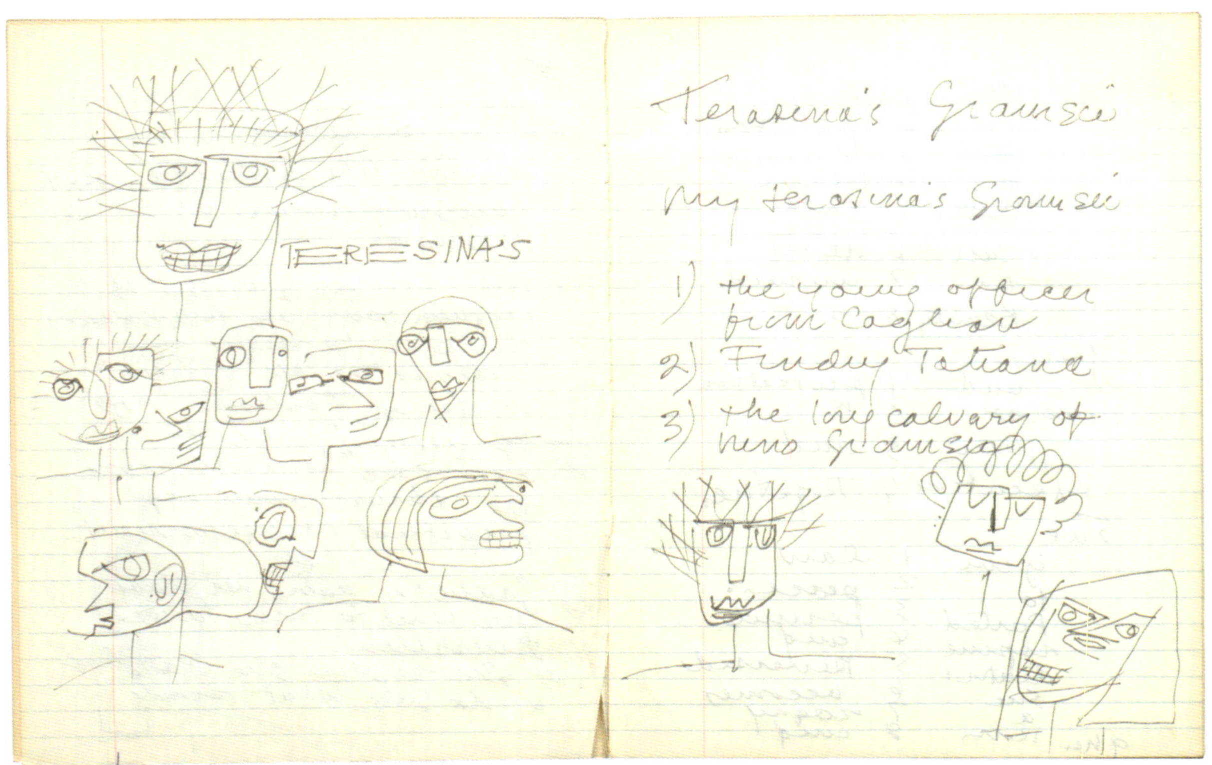

Watson's drawings of Teresina and other characters in *Gramsci x 3* (91-512)

Works Cited

Anonymous. Review of Wilfred Watson, *Friday's Child. The Listener,* XIV.1387 (Sept 29 1955): 515.

Arcand, Lucien. *Charles Dullin.* Paris: L'Arche, 1952.

Betts, Gregory. *Avant-Garde Canadian Literature: The Early Manifestations.* Toronto: U of Toronto P, 2013.

Cavell, Richard. *McLuhan in Space: A Cultural Geography.* Toronto: U of Toronto P, 2003.

Daniells, Roy. "Literature: Poetry and the Novel." *The Culture of Contemporary Canada.* Ed. Julian Park. Ithaca: Cornell UP; and Toronto: Ryerson P, 1957.

Dragland, Stan. "Apocrypha: An alphabetical sampler." *The New Quarterly* 19.3 (Fall 1999): 5–39.

Eliot, T.S. "Tradition and the Individual Talent." In *The Sacred Wood: Essays on Poetry and Criticism.* 1920; London: Methuen, 1960: 47–59.

Fiore, Guiseppi. *Antonio Gramsci: Life of a Revolutionary.* Trans. Tom Nairns. New York: Dutton, 1971.

Flahiff, F.T. *Always Someone to Kill the Doves: A Life of Sheila Watson.* Edmonton: NeWest P, 2005.

Gordon, W. Terrence. *Marshall McLuhan: Escape into Understanding.* Toronto: Stoddart, 1997.

Joll, James. *Gramsci.* Glasgow: W. Collins, 1977.

Lorelle, Yves. *Dullin-Barrault: L'éducation dramatique en mouvement.* Paris: Éditions de l'Amandier, 2007. Citations are the editors' translation.

Marcel, Gabriel. *The Mystery of Being.* 2 vols. Trans. René Hague. London: Harvill P, 1950, 1951.

Marchand, Philip. *Marshall McLuhan: The Medium and the Messenger.* Toronto: Random House, 1989.

McLuhan, Marshall with Wilfred Watson. *From Cliché to Archetype.* New York: Viking, 1970.

McLuhan, Marshall. *The Gutenberg Galaxy: The Making of Typographic Man.* Toronto: U of Toronto P, 1962.

McLuhan, Marshall. *The Mechanical Bride: Folklore of Industrial Man.* New York: Vanguard P, 1951.

McLuhan, Marshall. Marshall McLuhan Fonds. Library and Archives Canada.

McLuhan, Marshall. *Understanding Media: The Extensions of Man.* New York & Toronto: McGraw-Hill, 1964.

Mourges, Odette de. *Metaphysical, Baroque and Précieux Poetry.* Oxford: Clarendon P, 1953.

Powe, B.W. *Marshall McLuhan and Northrop Frye: Apocalypse and Alchemy.* Toronto: U of Toronto P, 2014.

Tiessen, Paul. "'Shall I Say, It Is Necessary to Restore the Dialogue': Wilfred Watson's Encounter with Marshall McLuhan, 1957–1988." *At the Speed of Light There is Only Illumination: A Reappraisal of Marshall McLuhan.* Ed. John Moss and Linda M. Morra. Ottawa: U of Ottawa P, 2004.

Tiessen, Paul. "Wilfred Watson, Playwright: Writing (to) McLuhan." *Counterblasting Canada: Into the Social and Intellectual Vortex of Marshall McLuhan, Sheila Watson and Wilfred Watson.* Ed. Paul Hjartarson, Gregory Betts, Kristine Smitka. Edmonton: U of Alberta P, forthcoming 2015.

Watson, Scott. *Jack Shadbolt.* Vancouver and Toronto: Douglas & McIntyre, 1990.

Watson, Sheila. *Sheila Watson Fonds.* Kelly Library, St. Michael's College, U of Toronto. Citations from the Sheila Watson Fonds are by permission of Sheila Watson's literary executor, acting on behalf of the Estate of Sheila Watson, and of the Archives, Kelly Library, St. Michael's College, University of Toronto.

Watson, Wilfred. *The Baie Comeau Angel and Other Stories.* Edmonton: NeWest P, 1993.

Watson, Wilfred. "The Canadian Fact." *white pelican* 2.1 (1972): 53–63.

Watson, Wilfred. *I Begin with Counting.* Edmonton: NeWest P, 1978.

Watson, Wilfred. "Interstructuralization in Drama and the Other Arts." *Thought: From the Learned Societies of Canada 1961.* Toronto: W.J. Gage, 1961. 15–22.

Watson, Wilfred. "McLuhan's Wordplay." *The Canadian Forum* LXI.709 (May 1981): 10–12.

Watson, Wilfred. "NGV as notation." *Mass on Cow Back.* Edmonton: Longspoon P, 1982: ix–xiv. This is an abbreviated version of "NGV as notation" published in *Open Letter* Fifth Series #2 (Spring 1986): 85–96.

Watson, Wilfred. "Over Prairie Trails to the Just Society." *white pelican* 2.1 (Winter 1972): 53–63.

Watson, Wilfred. "Place Marie Dialogues: Marshall McLuhan and Multi-consciousness." *Boundary 2* (Fall 1974): 197–211.

Watson, Wilfred. *Plays at the Iron Bridge, or, The Autobiography of Tom Horror.* Ed. Shirley Neuman. Edmonton: Longspoon P and NeWest P, 1989.

Watson, Wilfred. *Poems: Collected/Unpublished/New.* Edmonton: Longspoon P and NeWest P, 1986.

Watson, Wilfred. "The Preface: On Radical Absurdity." *Canadian Literature* 30 (Autumn 1966): 36–44.

Watson, Wilfred. "Wail for Two Pedestals: A Farce in Three Acts." *The Humanities Association Bulletin.* XVI.2 (Fall 1965): 61–92. Includes unacknowledged drawing by Norman Yates.

Watson, Wilfred. *Wilfred Watson Fonds.* University of Alberta Archives, University of Alberta, Edmonton. Citations from the Wilfred Watson Fonds are by permission of Wilfred Watson's literary executor, acting on behalf of the Estate of Wilfred Watson, and of the University of Alberta Archives.

Whittaker, Robin C., ed. *Hot Thespian Action! Ten Premiere Plays from Walterdale Playhouse.* Athabasca UP, 2008.

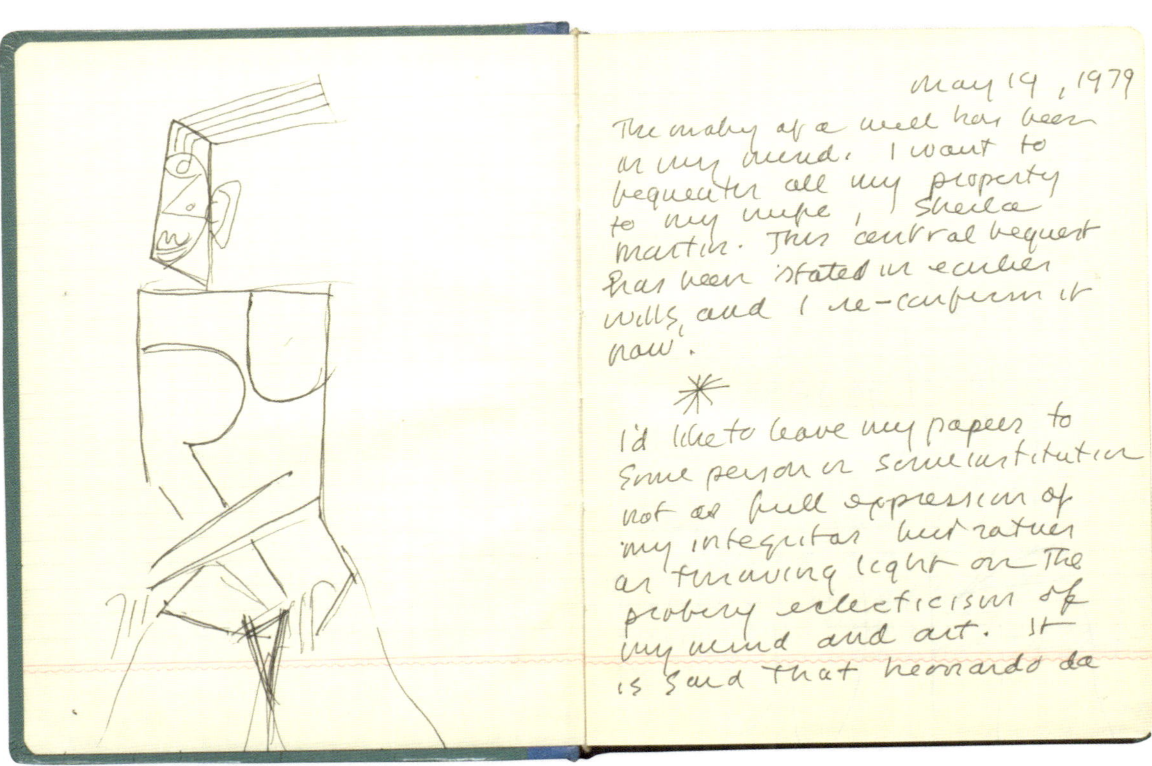

May 19, 1979

The making of a will has been on my mind. I want to bequeath all my property to my wife, Sheila Martin. This central bequest has been stated in earlier wills, and I re-confirm it now.

*

I'd like to leave my papers to some person or some institution not as full expression of my integritas but rather as throwing light on the probing eclecticism of my mind and art. It is said that Leonardo da

"The making of a will has been on my mind"; journal entry May 19 1979 (91-238).

Facing page:
Watson, drawing himself in the B.C. forests, a year after returning "home" (91-271 July 1981)

Acknowledgements

WE OWE LARGE DEBTS to two scholars who were the first to consult Wilfred Watson's papers: Fred Flahiff, who studied them for his life of Sheila Watson; and Paul Tiessen, for his work on modernism and new media. Flahiff's book is essential reading for any scholar of Wilfred or Sheila Watson's writing, not only because of his careful scholarship but also because of his many personal insights. Shirley Neuman, in particular, owes a great deal to Fred Flahiff for many years of conversation about both Wilfred and Sheila Watson. That conversation has shaped much in her own understanding of their lives, their relationship, and their work, and has added a good deal of information to that available in their archives. Paul Tiessen shared his transcriptions of the McLuhan–Watson correspondence with us. Without these, and without his essays on the collaboration between Watson and McLuhan, our work would have been more difficult and more tentative; we warmly thank him for his generosity and his insights. We also owe a large debt to Diane Bessai, colleague and good friend of Wilfred and Sheila Watson at the University of Alberta, who played a significant role in developing the study of Canadian theatre, particularly prairie and Edmonton theatre, and who wrote a pioneering entry on Watson. Our work builds on her efforts.

As every scholar in the archives knows, the pleasure of our work depends on archivists. We are much indebted to Raymond Frogner and James Franks at the University of Alberta Archives; to Gabrielle Earnshaw, Jessica Barr, Danielle Robichaud, and Kate Van Dusen in Special Collections and Archives at the John M. Kelly Library, St. Michael's College, University of Toronto; and to Robert Fisher, H. Marshall McLuhan Fonds, Library and Archives Canada. All have been warmly helpful at various stages of our research. The Wilfred Watson Exhibition builds on the labour of Editing Modernism in Canada research group members at the University of Alberta (EMiC UA), from those who have scanned the almost 100,000 pages in the Wilfred Watson Fonds or written back-up code, to those who have transcribed hand-written letters and chased down biographical and textual details. We should like, in particular, to acknowledge the work of Matt Bouchard, Andrea Johnston, Harvey Quamen, and Nick Van Orden.

The exhibition also builds on EMiC UA's ongoing partnership with the University of Alberta Libraries: we are housed in the Digital Initiative Centre, Cameron Library, where we work with, and receive invaluable support from, leading experts in the field. We should particularly like to acknowledge the assistance of Geoffrey Harder, Peter Binkley, Peggy Sue Ewanyshyn, and Peel's Prairie Provinces bibliographer Robert Cole. The exhibition itself was made possible by Head Librarian Robert Desmarais and his staff in the Bruce Peel Special Collections Library. Robert Desmarais has been most helpful and accommodating in seeing the catalogue into print.

We also want to acknowledge with thanks the following for permission to quote materials in archives: the Estate of Wilfred Watson and the University of Alberta Archives; and the Estate of Sheila Watson and the Archives of the Kelly Library, St. Michael's College, University of Toronto. Paul Hjartarson would like to acknowledge with thanks funding from the Social Sciences and Humanities Research Council and from the Killam Trusts.

Watson's drawing of the spit of land he named "Cow Back," visible from his home on Piper's Lagoon (91-290).

authors

PAUL HJARTARSON is Professor Emeritus in English and Film Studies at the University of Alberta. His scholarly work is on life-writing, Canadian literature, modernism, print culture, and the digital humanities. He leads the Editing Modernism in Canada research group at the University of Alberta (EMiC UA). In partnership with the University of Alberta Libraries (UAL), EMiC UA is developing a digital archive of Wilfred Watson's literary papers. With UAL, SSHRC Postdoctoral Fellow Hannah McGregor, and Faye Hammill, Professor of English, University of Strathclyde, EMiC UA is also developing the Modern Magazine Project Canada.

SHIRLEY NEUMAN is Professor Emeritus, University of Toronto. Sheila Watson's student over many years and through three degrees, she taught in the Department of English, the Department of Comparative Literature, and the Programme in Women's Studies at the University of Alberta from 1976 to 1996. Her scholarly work has been on theory of autobiography, feminist theory, Modernism, and Canadian literature. With Frederick Flahiff, she is now editing Sheila Watson's journals. She was a member of the founding editorial board of both NeWest Press and Longspoon Press and saw Wilfred Watson's last five books into print.